compassionate economics

The social foundations of economic prosperity

A personal view

Jesse Norman

University of Buckingham Press

First published in December 2008 by Policy Exchange
and The University of Buckingham Press Ltd

Policy Exchange
Clutha House
10 Storey's Gate
London SW1P 3AY

www.policyexchange.org.uk

Distributed by
The University of Buckingham Press
Buckingham MK18 1EG
+44 1280 828338

www.ubpl.co.uk

ISBN 978-1-906097-26-4

Designed by Soapbox, www.soapboxcomunications.co.uk

Contents

The ideas of economists and political philosophers, both when they are right and when they are wrong, are more powerful than is commonly understood. Indeed the world is ruled by little else. Practical men, who believe themselves to be quite exempt from any intellectual influence, are usually the slaves of some defunct economist. Madmen in authority, who hear voices in the air, are distilling their frenzy from some academic scribbler of a few years back.

John Maynard Keynes, *General Theory of Employment, Interest and Money*

Introduction

*The situation was aggravated by ignorance. The [local savings banks] had not been stress-tested for the bond market. They didn't know the mentality of the people they were up against. They didn't know the value of what they were selling. In some cases they didn't even know the terms of their own loans. The only thing they knew was how much they wanted to sell. The truly incredible thing about them, noted by all the Salomon traders, was that no matter how roughly they were treated, **they kept coming back for more.** They were like ducks on a corporate hunt trained to fly repeatedly over the same field of hunters until shot dead. You did not have to be Charles Darwin to see that this breed was doomed.*
Michael Lewis, *Liar's Poker*

In September and October 2008, in the words of the Governor of the Bank of England, the world's financial system came closer to collapse than at any point since the First World War.

Such a failure forces us to reflect: on its causes, and on its implications. Potboiling books of popular finance will denounce capitalism as such. Learned studies will be written analysing the sudden seizing-up of the interbank lending market, the failure of the money markets, and the dangerous interaction between financial innovation, complexity and globalisation. Commentators will endlessly opine.

But we can say this much already. At its deepest level, the crash arose because people and markets did not behave in the standard way described in the economic textbooks. First, people are not always economically rational: in this case, they massively overborrowed to buy houses, and then remortgaged those houses to buy other things. Second, free markets are not always efficient: in this case, they mispriced credit as banks hyped 125% mortgages and other debt products to a credulous public, then mispriced it again as the wholesale markets were unable to work out how much different mortgage assets were worth, leading to the wholesale equivalent of a run on the banks. And finally, poorly conceived policy and poorly crafted institutions can fail: in this case, there has been a huge institutional failure within the regulatory system, and in government oversight of the economy. Thus at every level, the present crash has arisen because people, markets and institutions do not behave as the old textbooks would have us believe.

Textbook Economics

Now British government and the general public have become far more knowledgeable about economics since the 1970s. But they have grown up with a standard 1970s schoolbook caricature of what economics is, and of economic man as perfectly rational and self-interested. Keynes's famous dictum that "practical men … are usually the slaves of some defunct economist" has applied with a vengeance. Except in this case it is not one economist as such but a whole standard economic model that has enslaved them—and us.

This "economism" has had two disastrous effects. The first is political: it has massively reinforced a thirty-year trend to greater centralisation and micro-management within government. Under Labour large parts of Whitehall, and in particular the Treasury, have fallen into a narrow and technocratic view of society. The result has been an extension of the tax and benefits system to include nearly 70% of the adult population of this country; an obsession with setting and monitoring performance targets; and endless fiddling with programmes in response to new initiatives or political wheezes. Within the public sector as a whole, it has helped to create a culture of low innovation and low productivity.

Typically, a particular group of people will be identified as in need of a state "intervention". The group will be specified mathematically and modelled financially in terms of its income or assets. Finally, the economic incentives it faces will be tweaked by the Treasury through the tax and/or benefits systems, or through other public spending decisions.

This dismal economic gospel regards the human world as static, not dynamic: as a world of fixed social engineering, not one of creation, discovery and competition. It is almost certainly damaging both our economy and our society. Intellectually, as we shall show, it cannot be right. Yet it has its advocates. They can defend themselves by pointing at their mathematical models and asking, properly, for flaws in the reasoning. Until critics can explain what has gone wrong here, and why and how economics itself must be re-embedded within a wider social and cultural debate, they will lack the theoretical resources to implement an alternative political vision. This is the first task of *Compassionate Economics*.

The argument is not merely about politics, however; it is also about society itself. If the received understanding of economics within government is radically incomplete, how much more so is it within society as a whole. We have been brought up and are daily conditioned to think of human beings as the "agents" of textbook economics: as purely self-interested, endlessly calculating costs and benefits, and highly sensitised to marginal gains and losses. And part of the achievement of economists since Adam Smith is to explain to us why this is OK—how individual self-interest can become social well-being.

But a problem comes when this economic image feeds back into society: when it becomes our default picture of human motivation. For we secretly know this picture is wrong. We are aware that there are routine aspects of our daily lives like volunteering or philanthropy which it cannot properly explain. We know that there are virtues such as loyalty and long-term thinking which seem to run directly counter to it. We fret about the atomisation of society, the commercialisation of human culture and the narrowing of our expectations of others. We over-invest in half-baked prescriptions for happiness. We yearn endlessly for the things money famously cannot buy: love, friendship, joy. Yet without an alternative picture of what a human being is, we cannot free ourselves from our assumptions. This is the intellectual heart of the matter.

This book, then, looks at the sources of our social and economic weakness, at the process by which we came to misunderstand economics, and how we can fix the problem: in short, at the social roots of economic prosperity. It explains how an ancient theory of human flourishing can be used to develop a far richer conception of human character and well-being. And it shows how that conception can be used to guide public policy today, in the Britain of the 21st Century.

Contradictions and Challenges
In so doing, *Compassionate Economics* brings out some implicit contradictions within the New Labour project. Since 1997 ministers have talked endlessly

of personal empowerment, yet they have pushed through legislation which has often disempowered the ordinary citizen. They have talked of devolution where the reality has been one of centralisation of power in Downing Street, marginalisation of competing institutions and self-entrenchment by the political class. It is hardly surprising that trust within society is so low when British government has, in effect, such a low opinion of the British people. We need a radically new approach, and a far richer conception of humanity in the public mind. This is the second task of *Compassionate Economics*.

Yet there is a challenge here too for the centre-right. Since 2005 the Conservatives have correctly placed ideas of fraternity and social responsibility at the heart of British political debate. The often-repeated line has been that as Mrs Thatcher repaired our broken economy, so David Cameron's Conservatives must lead the process of repairing our fractured society.

This has not simply been a matter of generating new ideas or policies. At the deepest level, it has required the creation of a new political viewpoint: a rethinking of the basic categories of political debate, so as to be able to approach the whole spectrum of public issues and concerns anew, and in a fresh and intellectually authoritative way.

This process of rethinking is well under way. It has been conducted with great energy and engagement, and many people and institutions have played a part. However, with a few notable exceptions, the centre-right as a whole has had little to say about the foundations of economics. Much excellent work has been done to develop new policy ideas and to build credibility with economic commentators, with the City, with business and above all with the general public. This has played an important role in winning the balance of public trust for the Conservative party on economic issues for the first time in 15 years. But the basic categories and assumptions of conventional economics remain broadly unquestioned.

Yet the need to reassess our economic assumptions could hardly be greater. The world's financial markets have seen extraordinary recent disruption and turmoil. The UK is in recession. Economic issues are at the top of the political agenda, with inflation now at nearly 5%, huge rises in the cost of living, growth at a standstill, unemployment up and personal indebtedness at an all-time high. And there is also growing public suspicion and resentment at the effects of the global market economy on the lives of individual people, and at the restricted terms in which economic debate is conducted: resentment which can be seen in riots against globalisation, in anger at the spread of "clone-town Britain", in feelings of loss of national identity and local control, and in public concern at the spread of consumerism and a money culture. It seems to many people as though we are in the midst of a culturally unsustainable corporate capitalism, yet one to which there is no alternative.

And there is also a pressing political reason. Economic issues are rightly regarded as a crucial litmus test for those who aspire to government. This is where fine words must yield to hard decisions, and competing political priorities find their place.

Under Gordon Brown we have reached the limits of state control and top-down government. For their part the Conservatives are well advanced on a transformation in policy, based on ideas of social responsibility and fraternity. But as a country, we need something bigger—we need a new political economy. Fifteen years after Francis Fukuyama announced in *The End of History* that capitalism had won, we as a society still lack a principled intellectual basis for defining what kind of capitalism we want—or even a popular belief that genuinely different varieties are available.

The centre-right has a particular responsibility in this regard. Communism and socialism have failed. Many people have noted that the left in Britain has run out of ideas—temporarily at least. Yet our current corporate capitalism, despite its achievements, also has major weaknesses. As these become more manifest there is genuine danger of a backlash, not merely against the particular kind of capitalism we have at the moment, but against capitalism as such.

The need for new thinking from the centre-right on these issues is thus of genuine public importance. For far too long the casual assumption has been made that any corrections to textbook economics must be left-wing. But in fact it is deeply conservative to seek to correct mathematically pure theory so as to reflect how people actually are: the crooked timber of humanity. The centre-right should understand this, and claim ownership of these ideas.

So where now for compassionate conservatism? Must it simply choose between command-and-control and laissez-faire? Between caricature Brownism and caricature Thatcherism? The answer is No. But first we have to see what is at stake, and that means looking at the underlying issues in more detail. We start with the state of the British economy.

1: The British Economy: Miracle or Mirage?

We cannot solve problems with the same kind of thinking we used to create them.

Albert Einstein

Until relatively recently, the conventional wisdom about Great Britain was this: the British economy of the past two decades has been a huge success story. Gone are the days of boom and bust, as the country has enjoyed continuous economic growth since 1992.

Sure, there have been crises: there was the Asia crisis, the Russia crisis, the end of the dot-com boom, the terrorist attacks of 9/11, and the Iraq war. All of these were serious events, with serious consequences for the world economy. Yet although Britain was clearly affected by them, they did not stop or reverse its economic growth for even a single quarter. That record of uninterrupted economic expansion stretched over an astonishing 60 consecutive quarters.

However, the story runs on, it is not only Britain's economic growth that has been remarkable. Interest rates, which had been in the double digits only 15 years ago, fell in the mid-1990s and then stayed for over a decade at historically low levels. Inflation, which had been all but impossible to control for much of the 1970s and 1980s, turned into virtual price stability. Unemployment, the bane of Britain for much of her post-war history, was replaced by near full employment.

Finally, there has been internal change. The structure of Britain's economy has drastically shifted away from manufacturing and towards services. Unproductive and unprofitable "sunset" industries have declined, while new clean, creative and international "sunrise" businesses have grown rapidly. Financial services in particular have become Britain's most important success story. Since Big Bang, the City of London has become arguably the world's most successful financial hub. With all this spectacular transformation, Britain can claim to be one of the very first post-modern economies, ahead of her Continental European neighbours and competitors.

This picture has an interesting asymmetry. When the British economy was riding high, the reason was said to be far-sighted economic management. Now it is struggling, however, this is apparently due to forces outside the government's control. There has been a collapse of the US sub-prime lending market, rising oil and food prices, and a crisis in domestic and international financial institutions. If our economy now finally succumbs to recession, well, that is only to be expected in the face of global economic forces.

So much for the conventional wisdom. Some of it is true. But the bigger picture is more interesting, and far more problematic. As this chapter explains, the British economy has done far less well in recent years than we believe. The fundamental drivers of our long-term prosperity have become weaker, not stronger, over the past decade. But the deepest problem is that we are still locked in the wrong thinking altogether.

Treading Water

To return: contrary to the conventional wisdom, Britain's economic performance since 1993 flatters to deceive, in two ways. The first lies in the contrast with Britain's post-war economic decline. By the 1970s the country had fallen far behind its major competitors, after three decades of relative underperformance. So the change from struggling economy to economic leader in the 1990s looked spectacular.

But there is also the contrast with Britain's international competitors today. Of course Britain is more prosperous than it was twenty, thirty or forty years ago; but so is every other major industrial economy. The real question is how Britain has done in relative terms. When British politicians celebrate the country's growth record, they usually compare it with those of the big economies of the Eurozone, Germany, France and Italy. And indeed the UK has significantly outperformed those countries in GDP growth since 1992, the final year of the last UK recession. All in all, the UK economy has grown by about 50% since then in real terms, while the economic growth of the Eurozone was less than 40%.

Not bad, one might say. But look again. For one thing, the Eurozone's growth has been held back by Germany, its industrial engine, which went through a painful and expensive process of unification. But the real point is that the major Euro economies are quite unlike that of the UK, with more highly regulated labour markets, and a greater relative emphasis on manufacturing than services. For similar reasons, though there is every reason for UK policymakers to be nervous about the extraordinary growth and economic ambition of China, India or Brazil, it makes little sense to compare our economy directly with theirs.

No, the real comparison should be with countries with a similar cultural, political and economic background to this one, in particular the principal mature free-market economies in the OECD whose language is English: Australia, Canada, the United States, New Zealand and Ireland. **And every single one of these countries has grown faster over the past 15 years than Britain**. Canada grew by 59% in economic terms, the United States by 60%, New Zealand by 62% and Australia by 73%. Ireland's position is deceptive since it has had some catching up to do, but its growth record of 167% between 1992 and 2006 was over three times that of the UK. And in case you think Ireland is still a "developing economy", bear in mind that it now has a higher per capita GDP than the UK.

So the true picture looks like this: the UK economy has grown faster since 1992 than the sluggish economies of mainland Europe. But it has lagged behind those of other more genuinely comparable industrial nations. Our growth has been remarkable only for its mediocrity. Instead of an economic miracle, we have been treading water at best.

Unfortunately even this picture is too rosy. You can have national economic growth with no genuine improvement if it is just a result of more people working. Imagine an economy which doubled its GDP by employing twice the number of people: its GDP per capita would remain unchanged. The wealth of the average individual would remain exactly the same, and any talk of real economic growth would miss the point.

Something similar has happened to Britain over the past fifteen years. While the economy grew by around 50%, much of this growth simply occurred because there was an influx of people who enlarged the workforce, and of course also became consumers. An extra three million people found employment in Britain—roughly 10% of the total workforce.

Once this is factored in, it turns out that UK GDP per head has in fact only improved by 42% since 1992. In other words, the UK's growth record is even weaker than appeared at first sight, and only just above the growth figures of the "sclerotic" Eurozone. Our economic miracle is a mirage.

Four Booms

Economic growth is not everything, of course, even to economists. It also matters, for example, how it is achieved. How has the UK's economic growth over the past 10-15 years been achieved?

Again, the answer is not encouraging, from a long-term economic perspective. As many people are now coming to understand, the UK economy has been driven forward by four booms over the past decade: in government spending, in immigration, in house price inflation and in personal debt.

By way of backdrop, we need to recall that the period 1997-2007 was what Mervyn King, the Governor of the Bank of England, called the NICE—Non-Inflationary Consistent Expansion—decade. Worldwide monetary conditions were extremely favourable, with interest rates and headline inflation in the major industrial countries generally at post-war lows.

The low cost of borrowing has been a crucial backdrop to the four booms, for when money is cheap it is easy for individuals, and governments, to borrow. Thus the first boom—the massive ramp up in public spending after 2001—was financed not only by taxation, but by a large and counter-cyclical increase in government debt. Under normal circumstances the conventional wisdom is that the state should record a slight surplus in boom times to balance out the inevitable deficit when the economy slows down. There was a surplus between 1999 and 2002, but since then the government has run a deficit, even without including the effect of public sector pensions and PFI debt. Indeed, we have seen a budget deficit of 3% of GDP at a time when the economy was still growing at nearly 3% a year: a clear sign that the country's finances have not been in balance. Since the financial crisis and the government's bail-out of the banks, this budget deficit has significantly worsened.

The growth in government spending helped to ramp up domestic demand and economic activity. And the economy was further supported by
a second boom, in immigration. When the UK opened its labour market
to workers from Poland and other East European countries in 2004, it
offered an unmissable opportunity. The Polish zloty was weak against the
pound, while wages in Britain were on average seven times higher than
in Poland. The Poles were well-educated, many spoke English and there
was a large young population of skilled workers willing to relocate. As a
result, an estimated 500,000 came to the UK. As well as pushing up GDP
they added to domestic demand, while their relatively low pay helped to
keep down reported inflation.

However, the boom in immigration has been dwarfed by our third
boom, in housing. Housing is the only area of the UK economy in which
price inflation is actually welcomed—but only of course by those already
on the housing ladder. The fundamentals of the UK housing market encourage this inflationary trend: in particular the lack of land supply, due in
part to strict planning controls and a system of local government finance
which discourages local development. Taken with significant population
growth, low interest rates and an explosion in credit, the effect between
1992 and 2007 was to push house prices up to astronomical levels. House
prices more than doubled in real terms over this period. Excessive mortgages of 100-125% of value became commonplace. Banks were only too
willing to lend people five or six times their salary; and even more if they
were prepared to 'self-certify' their own financial circumstances.

House price inflation soon became a self-fulfilling prophecy, and over time
the UK economy increasingly came to be built around it. One crucial effect
of this was to erode further the nation's already-weakening desire to save. In
the early 1990s UK households still saved about 8% of their disposable net
income. They saved for all the reasons that people usually have when they put
money aside: to pay for a new car, to spend it on a future holiday, to have a
better life in retirement, or simply to have some reserves for a rainy day. This
positive trend changed in 2004. Since then UK households have had negative
net savings rates. The savings rate is now only 1.1%.

Many things have undermined the British desire to save, including the dot-
com boom and bust and a series of stock market and insurance scandals. But

the most influential by far has been rising house prices. Putting your money in the bank seemed less and less attractive to many people as house prices soared. Why get 2 or 3% a year on your savings account when you could get 7 or 8% in the housing market, and more if you leveraged up and took on extra debt? Thus did the housing bubble become further inflated. But many prospective buyers also felt they had little choice. As houses became more expensive, they had to stretch still more financially just to be able to afford a decent place to live, and this squeezed out saving still further.

The rise in asset values in turn fuelled a fourth boom, in personal debt. Historically, consumption rested on thrift: you had to save up over time in order to buy a car or a kitchen or a foreign holiday. But for many people in the 2000s, rising property prices seemed to make this kind of saving a thing of the past. Wasn't it much easier to borrow against the value of your house in the hope, nay expectation, of a further rise house prices?

In this way some £250 billion was withdrawn from the property market. Much of it, together with a huge amount of new unsecured lending, went straight into consumption. The UK became a nation of consumers who were more than happy to gamble in the property market and buy plasma TVs on credit. Personal debt soared to nearly £1.5 trillion. Average household indebtedness rose between 1997 and 2007 from £24,650 to £56,501. Where only twenty years earlier personal debt had stood at below 60% of GDP, in 2007 it was, for the first time in history, higher than Britain's entire annual economic output. Eighty per cent of it was secured on private property. The credit crunch, when it came, fell upon an economy that was already hugely indebted and overstretched.

Ignoring the Fundamentals

Britain has not, then, experienced an economic 'miracle' since 1997, or even 1992. The economy has been sustained by easy monetary conditions, and by four huge economic stimuli in particular. Far from abolishing the normal cycle of boom and bust, the government has presided over a huge expansion in demand which has only served to defer economic reality, and perhaps to worsen its effects.

This would matter less if there were reason to think that the foundations of our economic prosperity—such as our national productivity, our institutional and legal framework, and above all our educational system—had been greatly strengthened. But here yet again there is real cause for concern. The truth is that none of these four booms has made much difference to the fundamental drivers of wealth creation in this country. Indeed, on the whole their effect may even have been to weaken those drivers.

The total increase in government spending over 1997 levels in the period since then has been of the order of £1.2 trillion pounds. If this sum had been used in part to provide the UK with world-class education or a world-class transport infrastructure over the past decade, for example, that would be one thing. If our rates of innovation and productivity had significantly risen during this period, that would be another. But they have not. We are still discussing the same problems today that we were ten years ago. The structural weaknesses of the UK economy have remained. And the most fundamental problems of our economy, and our society, cannot be solved by more money alone.

Moreover, these four booms have been episodic in character. They have washed through the British economy with relatively little positive legacy. We have already seen their disastrous effects on personal debt and on our savings habits. But consider immigration, which is often considered a great economic success story, again. Recently the pound has fallen dramatically against the zloty, while Poland has experienced strong economic growth. So the huge flow of hard-working, qualified Polish migrant workers of the past few years has ebbed away, and may now have gone into reverse. Many people now have new kitchens and house extensions as a result. But there is also reason to believe it has encouraged a long-term de-skilling of British workers in manual trades, who have been squeezed out by the temporary competition from abroad. It is notable that a recent bipartisan House of Lords study found "no evidence … of significant economic benefits" from recent immigration.

Meanwhile, the warm glow of apparent economic success has disguised the fact that the UK has almost certainly become less economically competitive over the past decade. A recent World Bank study placed the UK top as a place to do business in only one category—ease of obtaining credit.

But, one might ask, how can this be? How can 15 years of prosperity have failed to make us more competitive? There are many reasons. But the elephant in the living room is the growth and impact of the state. Public image notwithstanding, the Thatcher and Major governments in fact made almost no net impact on the size of the state, which in 1997 stood at about 36-37% of GDP consumed in taxes. Since 1997, however, the size of the state in Britain has grown fast. It is now projected to cost 45% of GDP in taxes in 2010, a rise of about one-fifth in 13 years.

But this huge expansion conceals a deeper continuity: the increasing centralisation of the state over the past three decades. Simon Jenkins has shown in vivid detail how deeply centralised British government became during the 1980s. To be sure, privatisation reduced state control of industry. But the public services — including primary and secondary schools, the NHS, local government funding and administration, the welfare state, the universities, the police — increasingly came for the first time under the direct sway of Whitehall, and in particular the Treasury.

Of course in many ways what Britain needed in the 1980s was strong government. But this centralising tendency has been grossly magnified under Labour, and in particular the creation, presentation and implementation of domestic policy have been concentrated in the Treasury under the chancellorship of Gordon Brown. Outside the Ministries themselves, a huge quangocracy of unelected bodies has arisen exercising public power on behalf on ministers, but with minimal accountability to Parliament. In August 2007 it was revealed that government spending on quangoes has risen by 700% since 1998.

Tax-financed expenditures have been estimated to have a negative economic impact on real GDP growth of between 0.14% and 0.25% each year. Even the lower figure would imply a drag on growth of just over 1% a year from the increased size of the public spending burden between 1997 and 2010. In the UK, moreover, it is almost certainly true that the public sector is pulling down national productivity — the ability to get more output for a given input. Rising productivity is absolutely fundamental to long-term economic growth. But in this country productivity growth has weakened over the past 10 years. It now lags behind that of most of the major Anglophone and EU countries. This is in striking contrast is with the USA, which has had a productivity revolution over this period.

A further constraint has been that of foolish or unnecessary regulation. International surveys show that the legal burden of doing business
in Britain has significantly increased over the past ten years. Tolley's tax
manuals, the industry standard reference work, have increased in length
from 2,529 pages in 1997 to 7,838 pages in 2008. Huge amounts of new
legislation have been introduced in such areas as health and safety, employment law and planning, as well as within specific industries. Huge
and costly new industries of compliance and audit have arisen to monitor
and enforce this legislation.

A similar story can be told across the public sector. The education
system alone has seen ever-greater central control of the curriculum; a
huge increase in testing; and the proliferation of dozens of new quangoes, each with its own remit, staff, CEO and board and funding, each
seeking to justify itself through endless activity of often dubious value,
often overlapping with and contradicting the others. Public spending on
education has risen by £38 billion a year—thirty-eight billion pounds
a year—since 1997.

And to what result? The quality of school education in the UK appears
to have fallen, not risen, compared to other countries. We have slipped
far down the international league tables in education. For example, the
OECD's benchmark Programme for International Student Assessment
study found in 2006 that the UK ranked 24th among 57 nations for
maths, and 17th for literacy. In 2000, it was eighth in maths and seventh
in literacy respectively. Another fundamental driver of our prosperity has
been seriously weakened.

The Unholy Alliance
Yet there is another and more subtle phenomenon also at work. This lies
in an unholy alliance between these centralising trends and the understanding of economics to be found in British public administration. This
understanding is revealed both in the behaviour of government and in
a series of explicit background papers on economic analysis such as the
Treasury's *Green Book: Appraisal and Evaluation in Central Government*.
What they show, broadly speaking, is that British government is in the
grip of an outdated 1970s textbook conception of economics.

It is this textbook approach that underlies and legitimates many of the policies and much of the centralisation and state growth that are weakening our economy. It has the effect of making the present government's recent obsession with top-down tinkering and micro-management seem not merely legitimate, but positively required. And at the same time, as we shall see, it has encouraged a politically useful belief in unfettered financial markets, so that much wise, active and hands-on regulation of banks by practitioners has been replaced by a culture of box-checking.

This standard economics treats human beings as purely self-interested, endlessly calculating costs and benefits, and highly sensitive to marginal gains and losses. It is extremely mathematical, and canonically expressed not in language but in the equations of calculus and statistics. We will explore this way of thinking later, and we will analyse its strengths and weaknesses in detail. But the key point is that it exercises an undetected monopoly of policy ideas and policy tools in the minds of many of our top civil servants and politicians. And like all monopolies, this one has malign consequences.

Tax Credits: A Case Study

The present tax credit system is a perfect example of this bad thinking in action. The idea of a negative income tax was advanced as early as the 1960s by Geoffrey Howe, based on an original suggestion of Milton Friedman. It has been regularly considered by different chancellors since then and rejected, mainly on the grounds of complexity, before being launched in the form of tax credits by Gordon Brown as Chancellor in 2003.

Tax credits are means-tested payments, and so are geared to the recipients' income. As that income changes, it is inevitable that in some cases under-or overpayments will occur. But it makes a huge difference if the system chosen tops up income before or after it is received. If it is topped up afterwards, then a family may have too low an income for a period before the top-up. But if the tax credit gets paid in advance, then the system becomes far more complex and overpayments—and, since this is public money, the need for government to reclaim them later—become more likely. How to design such a system is, then, a political and administrative judgement call.

Various different overall approaches have been tried over the years in countries such as the US, Canada and Australia. So a large amount of previous experience and knowledge about tax credit systems was available. But as Chancellor Gordon Brown did not adopt any of these approaches. Instead he decided to innovate, and to create a new, predictive and so highly complex tax credits payments system of his own, managed not from the Department of Work and Pensions but from the small and administratively inexperienced Treasury itself.

The results have been disastrous. The House of Commons Public Accounts Committee found in 2008 that the Government had overpaid £6 billion in the first three years of the system operation. A total of £2.3 billion had been wasted—enough, for example, to maintain the current public subsidy to the Post Office network for some 15 years.

During this period overpayments affected 1.9 million families (roughly one-third of those involved), not the originally projected 750,000. Some of these families were then thrust into debt as the state attempted to recover the public money already paid out. And what was almost worse: the system was so open, indeed encouraging, to fraud and abuse that it was discovered that 200,000 more single parents claimed tax credits than the Office of National Statistics believe are in existence.

It might seem absurd to say that part of the problem with tax credits was that their creators had a poor understanding of economics. Yet it is true, and that reliance had three malign effects. The first was that they wrongly assumed that ordinary people would actually understand and be able to react rationally to the massive complexities of the new system—in other words, they assumed people were far more economically rational than they actually are. In fact, the system is so complex that even experts often have great difficulty in understanding it.

The second effect was to focus attention at the margin: not on the mass of people who would be helped in their lives by a simple policy, but on the smaller number of extra ones who would be helped, or helped more, by a more complex one. For the argument was made, if we are looking after the core, why not look after them too? After all, they had needs—often very serious ones—and the additional complexity involved did not register in the model and so had no quantifiable cost. And of course these extra people were also voters. But if these were helped, then why not target the next group, and the next…?

This is how a focus on marginal cases naturally tends to increase complexity, and woo the policymaker into error. Of course a balance needs to be struck. But complexity naturally breeds waste, and creates new temptation for people to defraud the system. Thus can an economic decision have unexpected social and moral side-effects.

The final effect of the standard approach was to create more disruption when, as many predicted, the system went wrong. In orthodox economics, people are assumed to have equal and opposite reactions to gain or loss. But research from the 1990s in behavioural economics suggests that actually this is not true. In fact people are generally loss-averse: that is, they have a greater desire (roughly twice as great) to avoid loss than to make profit. The tax credits system did not recognise this. It created unexpected losses for a huge number of people, when Government sought to reclaim previous overpayments from them. It thus made a significant, continuing and largely avoidable contribution to human suffering.

Bad policy is just one effect of textbook economics. There are many others, as we shall see. But first we need to look at the effect of this economic worldview not on government, but on society as a whole. This is the subject of the next chapter.

2: A Fracture in Society

She looked over his shoulder
For vines and olive trees,
Marble well-governed cities
And ships upon untamed seas,
But there on the shining metal
His hands had put instead
An artificial wilderness
And a sky like lead.

A plain without a feature, bare and brown,
No blade of grass, no sign of neighbourhood,
Nothing to eat and nowhere to sit down,
Yet, congregated on its blankness, stood
An unintelligible multitude,
A million eyes, a million boots in line,
Without expression, waiting for a sign.
WH Auden, *The Shield of Achilles*

Auden begins at the moment in the *Iliad* when Homer describes the shield that Hephaestus has wrought for Achilles, before Achilles' climactic battle with the Trojan prince Hector. On the shield are set forth the heavens, the ocean, scenes of farming and dancing, and two great cities. One city is at peace, with a wedding and a legal dispute in progress. The other is at war, under siege and with a battle raging. It is a supreme metaphor for society as a whole: for humanity and nature, for order and disorder, for reason and emotion, for law and the chaos of combat.

Yet in one respect at least, Auden betters it. For in his poem the opposite of order is not disorder, but emptiness: the fields denuded of crops, no life or love or wit or human purpose, individuals swallowed up in an aimless crowd. Society has lost its meaning. Homer has life and death, yet Auden's image of nothingness and utter vulnerability is the more chilling.

Current concerns about British society are far removed from Auden. Yet a deep worry is evident today, a kind of moral panic about where our society is headed and what it is becoming. It can be seen in concern about social indicators such as drug abuse and teenage pregnancy. It can be seen in a widespread fear that towns and cities are losing their local character and the whole country its distinctive national identity. It can be seen in a lack of trust, and in feelings that those in power are distant, unaccountable for their actions and unable or unwilling to lead. And it can be seen in a growing belief that basic values are being swallowed up in rampant materialism.

These worries do not lack evidence. For example, the UK underperforms other EU countries across a wide range of social indicators: we have had the highest drug use in Europe for a decade in almost every major category, including cocaine, amphetamines, ecstasy and cannabis. We have by far the highest levels of binge drinking of the larger European countries. We have the worst record for teenage pregnancy, and the highest proportion of children in houses without work.

The position of young people is an especially telling indicator of what the future has in store. A 2007 report by UNICEF showed Britain near the bottom of 21 countries in the material and educational wellbeing of children; and lowest of all in self-esteem, unhealthy behaviour and quality of family and peer relationships. A further study found that more than 1.2 million 16-to 24-year-olds in England, Scotland and Wales, or just under one in five, are not in employment, education or training (NEET). In the 16 to 19 age bracket, the figure is 11%—twice that in Germany and France. Most recently, it was reported that one in ten children under the age of five is obese.

To make matters worse, these social problems do not fall evenly on the population. In general, the poor fare worse than the rich, the sick worse than the healthy, the old (and very young) worse than the young, those from ethnic minorities worse than whites. Social decline is thus highly socially regressive, compounding the effect of growing wealth and income inequalities. But all have been affected to some degree: a major poll by

The Observer in May 2007 revealed that on balance respondents believed that Britain in 2007 was less successful, less pleasant, more dangerous, less liberal and a lot less happy than in 1997.

In response to these problems, the British government has not distinguished itself either by policy or action. On the contrary, in social as well as in economic policy, the malign effects of recent state growth and centralisation are evident. They often stand in the way of better public services, and they embody an often profoundly insulting attitude to the ordinary citizen.

Thus Britain now has an incredibly complex benefits system that people struggle to understand; a pensions system that often deters saving; police forces that increasingly face inwards and upwards to their political masters, not outwards to local communities; a housing system that is slanted towards smaller flats and less green space; schools that are losing their freedom to teach; and a criminal justice system that offers less and less access to justice for the victims of crime.

It has 4.2 million security cameras, more than any country in the world except Communist China. Some of the most basic rights of British citizens have been deliberately eroded, while host of new regulations encourage petty dishonesty and fraud. Social mobility has declined. Meanwhile, the number of young people not in employment, education, and training has risen by 40% since 1997, while 3.8 million more people have been brought into the tax system—2.7 million of them among the less well-off.

It is perhaps not surprising, then, that popular trust in government itself is at a record low. This is not just a matter of falling turnout in elections. What is of special concern is how this disengagement splits broadly along the lines of age, ethnicity and income. In the 2005 General Election, only 37% of 18-24 year-olds voted, as opposed to 75% of those over 65. Among those of black or ethnic minority background, 47% voted; among whites, 62% did. Among those categorised in social classes D and E, 54% voted; among those in classes A and B, 70% did.

Contrary to much received wisdom, for these groups the point is not the supposed difficulty of voting. Nor is it simply that voters do not care about the issues of the day, since single-issue politics continues to flourish. No, the question for many people is whether it is worth voting at all. It seems as though the basic social contract—the implicit deal by which people trade social engagement for security—is starting to fall apart. Instead of elected representatives, they see a homogeneous political and media class which has lost its democratic connection with ordinary voters; and so lost the political legitimacy and authenticity which democracy creates.

The Discontents of Capitalism

Yet fears of social decline are not the only causes of loss of trust. Public concern runs far wider than this, to include feelings of loss of place, of value, of accountability and control. Walk through almost any city or town today and you see the effects of "clone town Britain", where high streets have been replaced by malls or superstores, and individual shops by a monochrome strip of global and national chains: one might be anywhere. Local values, customs and traditions have been superseded by national sales programmes. And little local power exists to question or influence these changes, especially once they have occurred.

Many of these fears are reflected by and through the green movement, and focuses on the effects of a go-faster, have-it-all society: on stress, poor health, noise, traffic congestion, sprawl, fast food and pollution. This new awareness has massively raised people's grasp of their own costs to others and to the planet.

But even among those who care nothing for the environment, there is the sense that something is wrong: that in some way human identity and human character are being lost in the face of a Gresham's law in which a money culture displaces traditional priorities and higher values. And many people have been tempted to think that the deepest problem lies not in individual or even national actions, but in the system of global corporate capitalism itself. It is supposedly this system that exalts values of greed and acquisitiveness in people. It is this system that has liberated economic forces which now sweep across the globe. And against this system even nations are, it is believed, powerless.

This line of thought mistakenly assumes that there is only one variety of capitalism, as we shall see. But whether or not you agree with it, the motivating concern that human character is increasingly driven by greed and fear is important. We have already noted that British government suffers from a faulty understanding of economics. But this is also true of our fundamental grasp of human behaviour. As a society we increasingly seem to believe that human beings are basically economic, rather than social, animals: that their behaviour is always motivated, and so to be explained, by self-interest and the desire for gain. On this view, people are calculating machines, always assessing the odds and the possibilities for gain. They always want more wealth, power and status. And so they fix their attention on the margin, where net cost yields to net benefit.

This view of human beings is very seductive, and in recent decades it has received huge cultural reinforcement from a wide range of sources. The media have endlessly promoted it, as though football transfers and Big Brother were the only form of human interaction. But most of all it has fed off itself. For once people start to see each other as merely economically or financially motivated, they treat them so. And once they are so treated, they themselves will tend to behave in the same pounds-shillings-and-pence way. And so it goes on.

But two other factors have also played a role. The first is the simple point that any action can in principle be "explained" through self-interest. Why do people act altruistically? Not because they want to help others, but because it makes them feel good. Why are soldiers prepared to die in battle? Not because they believe in a cause, but for personal prestige or family glory. Why did that politician do that? Not because of her character or ideals or sense of vocation, but because she's on the take. All very convenient—although a theory that purports to explain everything in fact explains nothing.

But confusingly, the self-interest view can also of course offer genuine and useful explanations. Everyone behaves selfishly sometimes, and some people do so often. Even more confusingly, it can often explain, and occasionally predict, aggregate human behaviour very well. That's what so much of modern economics is about, after all.

Nevertheless, as a default view of human motivation, the self-interest view is profoundly and dangerously inadequate. But first we need to get clear on how it arose in the first place. How did we get here? How did this economic idea of humanity achieve its present cultural pre-eminence and status in the public mind?

Enter Homo Economicus

The basic thought that people are purely economically self-interested goes back to the Epicurus and the ancients. But its present status is the creation of the last three centuries. It arose from the professionalisation of economics as an academic discipline.

Economics was more or less started by Adam Smith and the *Wealth of Nations* in 1776. But it was not invented by Smith. Rather, he created a systematic account from many already-current economic arguments and ideas. For example, most people would probably associate the words "laissez-faire" with Smithian economics. But in fact they were coined by Mirabeau and it was the French physiocrats, first and foremost François Quesnay, who developed many of the key economic ideas of the time. Smith's genius lay in bringing these ideas together and uniting them in a new body of thought.

Smith may have been the first modern economist, but he did not regard himself as one. Rather he saw himself as a moral philosopher, as a legal scholar and (in effect) as a social scientist. Thus he dealt with economic problems and ideas, but only in their wider social, historical and political contexts. And he certainly did not believe that human beings were purely selfish. Indeed he wrote *The Theory of Moral Sentiments* in 1759 to argue for the quite different and opposed view that sympathy or so much compassion was the psychological basis of personal morality.

The Theory of Moral Sentiments opens with the following lines:

> *How selfish soever man may be supposed, there are evidently some principles in his nature, which interest him in the fortunes of others, and render their happiness necessary to him, though he derives nothing from it, except the pleasure of seeing it. Of this kind is pity or compassion, the emotion we feel for the misery of others, when we either see it, or are made to conceive it in a very lively manner.*

In the Smithian view, personal morality and social norms arise from a process of imagining and reconstructing the experience of others. What matters is not compassion as pity, but compassion as fellow-feeling. Of this view the present book, and its predecessor *Compassionate Conservatism,* are distant, modest but direct descendents.

To return. For more than a hundred years after Smith, the greatest economic thinkers came from a wide variety of backgrounds: David Ricardo was a stockbroker, Leon Walras a mathematician, William Stanley Jevons a natural scientist, and Carl Menger a lawyer. The last economist who had a comparable universal education was Friedrich Hayek, who trained as both a lawyer and an economist but also published in the areas of psychology and political philosophy. And it was Hayek who once memorably remarked that nobody can be a great economist who is only an economist.

Both intellectually and in practice, then, the earliest economic thinking was embedded in society, and nowhere is this clearer than in the works of Adam Smith himself. But one need only look at any of today's standard economics textbooks to see that something has drastically changed since then. In fact many modern economics textbooks look rather like introductions to physics or mathematics. They are full of formulae and graphs, they use words like "equilibria" and "elasticity", but they often shun any reference to historical, social or political facts. So what has changed? And why?

In the *Wealth of Nations* Smith had presented us with a verbal description of the workings of the market economy. This was published at a crucial point in British history, in which the scientific advances of the Enlightenment were being used to drive forward the Industrial Revolution. Economists looked with amazement at the new steam engines, at railways, at electricity. And they noted that economics had not built any steam engines or railways; indeed it could hardly point at that time to any major achievement at all.

The early economists, especially those coming from a scientific background, thus naturally looked up to the exact sciences. In particular they looked up to Newton's towering *Principia Mathematica*, which seemed the definitive statement of the laws of physics, and which expressed those laws in mathematical form in the manner of Euclid's geometry. So what was more natural than a desire to mimic the natural sciences, with their elegant mathematical methods, their rigorous measurements and their astonishing capacity for prediction? And this meant one thing above all: the full-scale deployment of the latest mathematical techniques.

Take markets, for example. In Adam Smith's work there are many analyses of markets and the different ways in which they work. Yet during the 19th Century such verbal accounts were increasingly thought to be insufficiently precise. Starting with the French mathematician Cournot, a concerted attempt was made to improve on this assumed inadequacy of Smith. The result of the work of generations of economists since then has been to introduce various mathematically specified characteristics which have to be present to make a market work in theory: that is, to bring supply and demand into an efficient equilibrium.

This mathematical tendency arose from and reinforced a desire to move economics away from the messy detail of commercial society, which was all but impossible to model in equations, and into the more congenial atmosphere of theoretical abstraction. And it was notably blessed by John Stuart Mill, who was the very exemplar of the 19th Century liberal public intellectual. Political economy, said Mill "does not treat of the whole of man's nature as modified by the social state, nor of the whole conduct of man in society. It is concerned with him solely as a being who desires to possess wealth, and who is capable of judging of the comparative efficacy of means for obtaining that end. It predicts only such of the phenomena of the social state as take place in consequence of the pursuit of wealth. It makes entire abstraction of every other human passion or motive." Thus were human emotion and human society abolished from economic thought.

This process of making economics more mathematical took a major step forward with the publication of Alfred Marshall's great synthesis, the *Principles of Economics*, in 1890. Yet although Marshall himself strongly believed in the importance of mathematical rigour, he also knew that graphs and equations would deter the average reader. For him mathematics was a short-cut, a heuristic used to reach results whose final expression must be in plain English using real examples.

In part as a result, Marshall's book was a huge success, whose influence stretched to the Second World War. And that success was repeated after the war by Paul Samuelson with his famous textbook *Economics* in 1948. *Economics* was a comprehensive presentation of broadly neoclassical economics from first principles. In many ways it updated, refined and extended the work of Marshall. Yet it also differed in two crucial ways. The first was in content. The interwar period had seen the triumph of John Maynard Keynes and his ideas of activist government. In his General Theory, and in his own role as government adviser, Keynes gave a master-class in showing how an economic theory, vigorously advocated, could have profound effects on policy.

According to the not naturally modest Keynes and his acolytes, his theory finally achieved what economists had long dreamt of. It explained the cause of the British interwar economic malaise, as too little demand in the face of huge unemployment, resulting in stagnation. But it also gave a prescription to government as to how to cure the problem, through large-scale state spending and conscious targeting of full employment. For its part, Samuelson's book showed how Keynes's ideas could be incorporated within a neoclassical framework. Thus was born a policy consensus that lasted until the 1970s, and a theoretical outline of economics that remains broadly in place in the public mind today.

One further interesting event deserves brief mention in this potted history. That is the publication of *The Calculus of Consent* by James Buchanan and Gordon Tullock in 1962. This book effectively launched what has become known as Public Choice theory, or the application of economic principles to political matters such as voting, the working of special interest groups and the behaviour of politicians. Its special significance for this discussion lies in two things. First, in the fact that it took much political explanation to be founded on the basis of economics; and second, in its assumption that politicians and bureaucrats, far from following any vocation or calling or devotion to public service as they often professed, were in fact purely economically motivated. Thus was politics logically subordinated to economics, and thus was the theoretical justification laid for centuries of voter disgust, before and afterwards, with politicians and public servants.

For his part, Paul Samuelson shared Marshall's passion for rigour. But unlike Marshall he saw himself as writing less for the common man and more for a (semi-) professional audience of undergraduates and academics. He was thus quite willing to use ideas, metaphors and techniques from mathematics and physics, which contributed to the sense that here was something privileged, expert and important. The overall result, reinforced by Samuelson's Nobel Prize in 1970, was a huge leap in the intellectual prestige and popular fame of economics as a subject. Universities widely adopted Samuelson's book, in the UK as in the USA; undergraduates scratched their heads and occasionally absorbed it; and some of those undergraduates became today's politicians, civil servants and policy wonks.

There is one other and more melancholy point of continuity. In their desire to present a comprehensive and unified synthesis of their subject, both Marshall and Samuelson downplayed the existence of dissident voices and competing points of view. The effect was to reinforce the sense of an orthodoxy within economics, and this in turn heavily shaped the research agenda and fed into tenure decisions within the universities.

The Return to Reality

Yet in fact 1970 was the high water mark, the point at which academic economic orthodoxy started to change, fragment and reassemble itself. It was almost exactly at this time that economics as a profession started to turn back to reality. True, the subject became ever more relentlessly mathematical. But the target changed: since then using economic theory to describe and predict actual human behaviour better has become a central preoccupation of the discipline. Well-known examples of this include Daniel Kahneman and Amos Tversky's use of cognitive psychology to explain common mistakes in human rationality, Gary Becker's extension of economics into sociology, crime and family dynamics, and George Akerlof's examination of the effect of asymmetric information on markets. But there are many others.

The present public understanding of economics, however, reflects few if any of these changes. On the contrary, it remains rooted in the textbooks of the 1970s. The present situation thus piles irony upon irony. The more mathematical economics became, the less well-understood it was by the average person whose behaviour it sought to explain. The less well-understood it was, the greater grew its prestige. The greater its prestige, the more people wanted to study it. A theory dedicated to explaining markets and competition achieved a virtual monopoly in its own marketplace. With every shift along this path, economic theory moved further away from the real world. And just at its apogee, at its point of greatest distance from human life in all its infinite variety, that standard economics entered British government and the British public consciousness. And there is has broadly remained, and grown.

In this worldview, as Mill wished, every contextual element has been purged from Adam Smith's original account. Time, place and people no longer exist. Reason is reduced to mere calculation. What remains is a perfect world, with perfect markets shaped by perfect competition: an economic version of Nirvana that has little if anything to do with the world we see around us every day.

Instead there is, in Auden's words, not olives, vines and well-governed cities, but *An artificial wilderness / And a sky like lead. / A plain without a feature, bare and brown, / No blade of grass, no sign of neighbourhood. / Nothing to eat and nowhere to sit down.* It is a towering technical achievement. But if our understanding of economics relies purely on it, then that understanding is grossly and dangerously deficient. Or so we shall argue.

3: Rigor Mortis Economics

Economics is the study of mankind in the ordinary business of life.
Alfred Marshall

Mathematics brought rigor to Economics. Unfortunately, it also brought mortis.
Kenneth E. Boulding

It's late afternoon. You're in the office and need to do an hour's more work. But the sun is shining and your friends are having a picnic. You know the beer is warming up with every passing minute. What to do?

Luckily, you have in the back of your mind a rather rusty PhD in neoclassical economics. That theory says that you will work up until the point when your benefit from more work is exactly counterbalanced by your loss at not going out with your mates. After sketching a few graphs, setting up a spreadsheet and using your trusty skills in calculus, you decide the tipping point is 5.47 pm. At that time, off you go.

OK, so the last bit is a caricature. But it reminds us that this kind of general thinking, trading off costs and benefits up to a marginal point where they are equal, is absolutely commonplace. We do it every day, in hundreds of different ways. And we typically do not think of it as economic thinking at all. It's just about planning and running our lives.

Conventional economics is in part a theory about how people make these decisions. We can think of it as making three key assumptions. The first is that people have perfectly rational preferences among different outcomes; this means, for example, that if they prefer A to B and B to C, then they prefer A to C. The second is that individuals maximise their utility, or gain, or benefit; and firms maximise their profits. And the third is that they act independently of each other, on the basis of perfect information. All of these have echoes in the example above.

The core assumptions, like those in the natural sciences, are idea-lised generalisations. They do not purport to describe what people are actually like, only to be useful simplifications. The idea is that people's differences balance themselves out in the aggregate, so that the theory looks to generate rich explanations and predictive power by treating people as if they were perfectly rational utility-maximisers operating under perfect information.

Now you often hear people say about this picture, with a knowing smile: "Ah yes, but it's completely flawed, because no-one is really like that". But this is no part of our standard economics as such. That is not a theory about how individual people actually are, only about how they behave overall. By analogy: for centuries after Newton, physics made the assumption that gravitational force was always exercised from a point at the centre of given body. It may or may not have been true, but it made for some stunning predictions. The really damaging criticism is not "no one is really like that". It is that even in the aggregate people systemati-cally do not behave as the standard model predicts.

Of course, people do not live in a vacuum; they constantly deal and trade with each other, through markets. And these markets use prices to show the relative scarcity of the goods and services traded. Prices are signals from people and households to firms to show what they want, and from firms to households to show how much those things cost. When supply and de-mand balance out, then a market is said to be in equilibrium.

But the greatest claim of the theory lies at the level not of the individual or the market, but at that of an economy as a whole. For economists have been able to show in a formal, mathematical way under certain very specific conditions that a market economy which is in competitive equi-librium is maximally efficient. Moreover, such an economy maximises the utility or benefit of the people in it. No-one can be made better off without someone else being made worse off. Adam Smith's invisible hand thus creates not merely the greatest aggregate efficiency, but the greatest overall utility as well. That's quite a result.

This approach has been filled out over time with detail, and with spe-cific tools. Two of these deserve mention: discounted cash flow analysis and cost-benefit analysis. Discounted cash flow analysis is a mathematical tool by which to estimate the value today of cash payments in the future, or vice versa. It reflects a standard assumption that capital sums and income streams can be treated equivalently. Cost-benefit analysis is a formal technique of project appraisal, which values the expenses and expected returns of a project in monetary terms to establish a net positive or negative contribution. Both approaches are extremely widely used within government and in the private sector. Within government they have been heavily promoted and exhaustively analysed, especially within the Treasury and within successive departments of the environment and health.

This, then, is the traditional picture. It has become our conventional economic worldview. In the economics profession it is often called the Standard Economic Model or SEM. If we needed an –ism we might call it economism, but *rigor mortis* economics is perhaps still better. As a formal theory it is a work of great beauty and genius. But it has many weaknesses. Much of its actual real-world value is illusory. Some of its consequences are positively dangerous. And its hold on the public mind is bunk. Economic theories are not religious monoliths but tools of explanation, prediction and policy. This textbook economics is not the only game in town. There are other theories, and other ways we should be thinking about people and their behaviour, yet to be considered.

And one point in particular is worth noting. The present picture implies that any derogation from perfect competition in a market economy creates inefficiency and makes some people worse off. So socialism must fail. But so too must rational debate about different varieties of capitalism. For on this account there can only be one, hyper-libertarian, variety of capitalism. In other words, just at the point when we need an intelligent debate about how the UK and other modern market economies should develop, our most basic economic theory seems to make that debate impossible.

Unpicking the Assumptions
In fact, however, the standard economic model is nothing like as robust as it appears. At its core is a set of ideas each of which has been severely questioned by professional economists over the past 30 years. But what is so striking is the intellectual hold which the standard model continues to exert on public policy and on British society as a whole. In this chapter,

then, we look more closely at the weaknesses of the standard model, and at its damaging effects – including its role in the recent financial crisis.

Perfect Competition?

We start with the analysis of markets. According to textbook economic theory, markets produce efficient results—but only if they fulfil certain formal criteria. There must be myriads of buyers and sellers, whose identity is unknown, each of whom is omniscient about market information and each too small to have an influence on the market price. What is traded on the market must be homogeneous, that is exactly identical: there can be no branding or even provenance such as "Jaffa orange juice", for example. These theoretical markets supposedly react instantly to any change in supply and demand, so that there are no processes that take place over time. In an economy, there is deemed to be a complete set of perfectly competitive markets, for all goods, everywhere and always.

In other words, these markets occupy no time and no place. Moreover, for the same reason, there are no human accretions in this picture: no institutions, no practices, no rules or traditions, no moral or ethical standards, no emotion, no human relations, no altruism or fellow-feeling, no philanthropy, no rule of law, no history, no culture.

However, many economics textbooks tend to use the model of perfect competition as a prescription for what markets ought to be. Take the latest edition of Samuelson's *Economics*, one of the best-selling economics textbooks ever written. After listing the requirements of perfectly competitive markets and claiming that only such markets can lead to efficient outcomes, they write: "Alas, there are many ways that markets can fall short of perfect competition … Market failure leads to inefficient production or consumption, and government can play a role in curing the disease." In other words, reality is seen through the spectacles of formal economic models. Discrepancies between reality and the idealised models are then seen as some sort of imperfection—but in reality, not in the model.

In the real world, of course, the key assumptions of textbook economics are rarely even closely approximated. But the effect of this formalisation is to exclude from the theory roughly all of the things that give human life its point and meaning. A world without culture is a world without music and joy. A world without moral standards is a world without personal obligation, regimental loyalty or human character. A world without institutions is a world without families, clubs and reunions. A world without emotion is a world without love or friendship or trust.

It is also a million miles away from Adam Smith. For Adam Smith, capitalism is not a form of desiccated economic atomism. He recognises the invisible hand, of course, but he also recognises the human capacity for sympathy or compassion. So he sees markets not as disembodied but as operating within a rich local cultural context which embraces individual moral standards, a person's own energy, flair and imagination, unstated background assumptions as to honesty and fair dealing, and a shared understanding of market conventions, institutions and traditions. In short, the Edinburgh of the 1770s.

Perfect Information?

We can go further. Part of the beauty of market economies today is precisely that they do **not** obey the assumptions of the standard model, and yet in many ways they still function remarkably well. Thus consumers do not need perfect information about goods traded in the market. On the contrary, they may know virtually nothing about them. But they can still generally rely on markets and the division of labour to meet their demand at a given price. Mrs Bloggs may not have tea plants or the steady sunshine of Darjeeling at her disposal. She may think tea is an oil by-product made by human slaves on the planet Venus. But if she has the right cash she can buy a pack of PG Tips whenever she chooses.

Not only that: there is reason to think markets actually require imperfect information in order to work properly. For if markets always contained perfect information, no-one would or could have an incentive to find out more. Similarly, if all technological insights were immediately available to others, no inventor would have an economic incentive to innovate, and innovation would cease. The effect of assuming perfect competition and market equilibrium is thus in fact to prevent any competition from taking place at all.

This is a major weakness in the conventional theory, because it strikes at the heart of a basic assumption about information. But its value does not cease there. For it also draws attention to the static, arrested nature of the theory as a whole. It suggests that there are no such things as equilibria in economics, as in nature; that everything is on the hop and in flux; and that markets in particular are dynamic, liquid movements that cannot be properly understood in static terms. In the real world, of course, this is not news.

Rationality, Behavioural Economics and the Financial Crash

These assumptions about markets and information are fundamental to the standard economic model. It would be silly to think that they would, could or should ever go unanswered. On the contrary, there has long been a flourishing trade within the academic world of economics in examining what happens when they are changed and deliberately imperfect assumptions are made instead.

The same is true for the standard assumption that individuals are perfectly economically rational, and the most important line of criticism for the present discussion targets this assumption. That criticism is largely based on behavioural economics, which draws on insights from human psychology. We saw earlier how standard economics wrongly assumes that people are equally geared to gain and loss, whereas in fact they have a disproportionate aversion to loss. Recent research has shown many other flaws in the assumption of perfect rationality. People systematically behave quite differently and more interestingly than the standard expectation would suggest.

We do not need to enter the laboratory to see evidence that humans are not fully economically rational. Consider the financial markets, which are often taken to be the paradigm of market activity. Even well-informed financial investors often behave irrationally. They get caught up in fads, they follow financial gurus, they obsessively chart price movements, they fail to diversify their portfolios and they churn their shares, for example. Markets can be inefficient, they can misprice risk and reward, and they can overshoot for reasons of fashion or sentiment on the way up or down.

But this is merely anecdotal. What is more interesting is research which shows that people are not randomly economically irrational, but follow fairly consistent patterns. Thus there is strong evidence that people are biased towards the present and *status quo*, even in the face of positive reason to change their view; that they cue their reactions off key reference points, rather than by systematically evaluating the alternatives; that they place a higher value on objects they own than on new ones; and that rather than seeing money as always and everywhere the same, or capital as simply equivalent to deferred income, they run their finances by thinking in terms of different pots of money or "mental accounts".

Not only that: how people take decisions is heavily influenced by the way those decisions are framed, so that they choose one option when a choice is framed positively and another when negatively. They also think of risk and reward in terms of available and salient examples, so that the probability of someone's dying in a tornado is rated higher than, say, from asthma (in fact in the US at least the latter is twenty times more probable). All of these types of behaviour violate the rules of rationality assumed by textbook economics. But few will come as a deep surprise to those who reflect on their own behaviour, or who have studied modern marketing techniques. For many of those techniques are designed to exploit precisely these features of human psychology.

There is now a huge literature on behavioural economics, much of which is directly relevant to public policy. The fact that people tend to think of money in different mental accounts, for example, is of great significance for future reform of the benefit system. But the key point is simply this: in the absence of definite information human beings often make very poor judgements about what to do.

The recent financial crisis makes the case perfectly. It seems likely that the housing boom was fuelled by a range of features of human psychology which encouraged buyers to make poor choices. On this view, individuals' natural bias towards the present inclined them to accept teaser mortgages from banks offering very low rates for an initial period but at a much higher later cost. As values started to rise, other buyers were cued or competitively encouraged to enter the market who would not have done so otherwise, even at the higher prices. They were further stimulated because of the known human tendency of people to overestimate their ability to save for the future, and through a ratchet effect whereby they find it easier to adjust their expectations upwards rather than downwards. Once the boom was established, owners' appetite for risk may also have risen because they were already sitting on large unrealised capital gains, fuelling further price rises.

Moreover, it may well be that the continuance of low interest rates created a perception that the world had in fact become less risky than it was. And above all there was also a competitive me-too instinct not to miss out on the boom, but keep up with others. As the groundswell of demand grew, any anchor which prices might have had in fundamental values dropped away, and it became in no-one's interest to question or attempt to correct further rises. The result was galloping and unsustainable house price inflation, and a disproportionately greater final crash.

Bad Influence, Bad Policy

Let us review the discussion so far. Both argument from first principles and recent empirical research suggest that the standard model is intellectually unsustainable. There is good reason to implicate it as a prime cause of the recent housing boom and bust. Yet it continues to exert its grip on our public administration and on the public mind.

But what are the effects of this mistaken economic picture on public policy? First, a disclaimer. In many ways the embedding of conventional economics within public policy has had a huge positive impact. Indeed it would be impossible to imagine any genuine UK policy discussion today without it. Compared to 30 years ago, there has been a transformation in the understanding of economics within government. It is no longer the main preserve of the Treasury, but also is widely shared within spending departments, quangoes and local government. The public economic statistics are far more comprehensive and transparent than they were. And the disciplines which sound economic management implies—of value for money, assessment of costs and benefits and the relative value of money now and in the future—are of huge importance.

Moreover, what matters is not just the overall theory, but the panoply of current conventional economics and tools, and the very confident approach to government, which it carries with it. It is far from easy to separate out economic ideas from political ideology or implementation. But part of our argument is precisely that there has been an unholy alliance between conventional economics and recent (mainly but not exclusively Labour) political ideology, and to explore why this should be. So this mixing-up is to be expected.

Centralisation and Control

Nevertheless, there is real cause for concern. The first point is that this standard economics is not politically neutral. Economists like to think that their discipline is just a tool, to be used in assessing all and any policy regardless of political coloration. But in fact this is not true. As we have seen, this view has no place for people, place and time. It assumes institutions do not exist. It specifically excludes all the paraphernalia and messy human relationships that make up civil society. When conventional economics is applied to policy, there are only two kinds of thing in its models: individual economic agents and the state. And among economic agents, the marginal ones matter more to policy-makers than those at the core.

The effect of this is to build in an unrecognised presumption in favour of centralisation, a top-down command-and-control mentality, and an obsession with interest-group politics at the expense of genuine leadership — precisely the approach to policy-making increasingly adopted by British government over the past two decades. To be sure, the Thatcher government had a certain tolerance for centralisation and impatience with existing public institutions, as we have seen. But it was operating, quite properly, broadly within the existing framework of cabinet government. What is so striking is how the situation has deteriorated under New Labour since 1997.

In his famous book *The Anatomy of Britain* Anthony Sampson noted that there was no single centre of power in Britain: rather, power was exercised through a network of institutions including parliament, the judiciary, the crown, the armed forces, the church, the media and the professions. But in conventional economics, as we have noted, there are no institutions at all. There are individuals and firms, and to them is added the state. Since 1997 New Labour has made a fairly systematic attempt to conform government to this pattern, and to disable alternative sources of power, as Peter Oborne and others have described. The result is that the state, and specifically Downing Street and the Treasury, have been more dominant in relative terms during the past decade than at any time in modern memory. But, crucially, they have been tacitly assisted in this task by some of our deepest and most widely shared intellectual preconceptions about the basis of policy itself.

Wrong Operational Model

This conventional economic worldview not only fuels a political tendency to centralisation and control. It also reinforces a bad operational model in government.

To understand the model, one must understand the problem it is designed to solve. Broadly speaking, for deep and long-term economic reasons services are progressively becoming more expensive, and more expensive relative to manufacturing. The manufacturing sector has massively systematised and proceduralised its operations. The service sector has not, because services offer relatively little scope for productivity gains. After all, ideally we would like nurses to spend more time with each patient, not less. This phenomenon of escalating relative service costs is known among economists as Baumol's cost disease.

The British state is a gigantic provider of public services, including the NHS and the education and welfare systems. So the effect of rising service costs, even before the impact of any waste and inefficiency, is to place unrelenting upward pressure on budgets and so on public spending. More and more money is needed to achieve the same outcomes.

Under Messrs Blair and Brown, the response of government has been to postpone the problem by spending massively more. But they also recruited a gigantic client state of consultants. These have tried to apply the supposed lessons of lean manufacturing to government in a coercive and standardised way, by creating so-called "public service factories". Services are specified from the centre; and departments split into front-and back-office functions, given targets, and made subject to inspection and compliance regimes. A focus on people is replaced by a focus on procedures. A silo mentality replaces a holistic view of a given public service as such. Trust is replaced by mistrust. A mania for quantification and cost control infuses the whole. And crucially, real demand for public services is overshadowed by what systems theorists call "failure demand"—the demands placed on an organisation by people whom it has failed to satisfy.

In recent years we have seen the same story played out again and again across the public sector, with a one-size-fits-all approach which ignores the nature of the institutions involved and treats public employees like cattle. The results are higher costs, lower morale and poorer services.

Misleading Rhetoric

Conventional economics, thus, predisposes us in the wrong ways both in the formation and implementation of policy. But its highly technical nature also requires it to be handled with extreme care. If not, it offers huge scope for manipulation. It is frequently used not to provide independent grounds for a decision but as a rhetorical means to persuade others of a decision that has already been taken for other reasons. The result is to diminish normal political processes of deliberation and accountability, and often to harm those who cannot afford the necessary external expertise.

Take cost-benefit analysis, for example. In the 1980s this was generally used as a specific tool to appraise relatively small projects which had ascertainable local effects. But this limited use has expanded massively since then to include huge issues and projects in which it is all but impossible to measure the relevant costs and benefits adequately. Even where these can be assessed in some way, it may be impossible to place a cash value on them, as the theory requires. And even when those involved agree that the relevant costs and benefits can be valued in cash terms, that value may prove to be infinite. The person who has lived all their life in the same house, or worshipped in the same church, may simply not wish to change under any circumstances. Yet a cost-benefit analysis with infinite costs cannot get started.

And there is a more subtle problem. Cost-benefit analysis normally assesses gains in terms of what those affected would be willing to pay to obtain them; and it analyses losses in terms of what payment those affected would be willing to accept to suffer them. This is partly for reasons of fairness: the idea is that the people who enjoy the gains and suffer the losses are the best judges of how much the gains or losses are worth.

But only rarely do the amounts gainers are willing to pay and losers to accept equal each other. Almost invariably, they do not. What then? Ultimately, side one must be preferred for the analysis to take place at all. And which one is chosen is not a neutral matter. Imagine the government is deadlocked with local green protesters over a new building project. If the question is what the protesters would be willing to pay to avoid damage to the local environment, this implicitly assumes a bias to development. It transforms rights that people used to enjoy into privileges for which they must pay. Conversely, if the question is what the protestors would accept to allow the development to proceed, then given people's status quo bias, this creates an implicit bias against development. In other words, lying within these abstruse and technical matters are assumptions which can often fundamentally change the basic terms of debate, and unconsciously influence the outcome.

Until relatively recently, the Treasury's *Green Book* only used the willingness-to-pay approach. It therefore carried with it an implicit bias in favour of development. But this, though important, is incidental. The wider point is that cost-benefit analysis and other formal mathematical tools are of far less value than currently believed, and seriously prone to abuse. Their value is often more rhetorical than real.

Bias Against Risk

The fourth and final effect concerns risk. Risk is always present in human society. We have already seen how it is often misjudged by individuals. But it is also very poorly understood by government. The result is that we all live less joyful lives. Why should this be?

We can think of risk as the possibility of gain or loss. People take risks in part because they want the gains that risk can bring: they drive fast in order to get somewhere quicker, they take drugs to get high, they go rock-climbing for the thrill of it. Occasionally, of course, they get the losses that come from risk and not the gains. But taking risks is not irrational. On the contrary, it appears to be both rational and an inevitable part of human nature.

Indeed, the evidence suggests that we each have a "risk thermostat"; that is, a default setting towards a certain level of risk. The setting will differ between people, and across a lifetime. But it adjusts to suit the circumstances. If we are taking too little risk, we naturally tend to adjust our risk-taking upwards. If too much, we tend to reduce it. Thus one of the unexpected consequences of the seatbelt laws has been to raise the speed at which cars are driven. Why? Because seat belts reduce the risk of serious accident. So drivers can go faster without any net increase in risk.

Now consider the matter from a public perspective. Accidents show up in the economic models as losses. But there is generally no quantification in cost-benefit analysis of the reward arising from any risks taken. Furthermore, as the state is extended into private life, the possibility increases that some public authority will be held responsible for an accident and attract criticism or, increasingly, litigation. The effect of this is that the state always seeks not to manage risk, but to reduce it.

But risk has rewards as well as penalties. So the inevitable result is a ratchet which pushes us towards bossy government, higher costs, greater paperwork and less joy. These effects are everywhere to see, in schools with over-engineered playgrounds but no new books; in an intrusive culture of official health-and-safety jobsworths; or memorably in the recent ban on undergraduates at Anglia Ruskin University from tossing their mortarboards in the air on graduation day, for fear of the safety consequences.

And there is also huge social frustration. A person who is unable to take their default level of risk in one way will find other ways to do so. A society which is systematically prevented from taking its desired level of risk will find itself deeply thwarted and unhappy. Yet this is what seems to have been happening in Britain in recent years.

It may seem fanciful to connect such things as the recent rise in drug abuse and knife crime with the social acceptance of a standard economic worldview. But the present line of thought suggests a clear linkage. Intriguingly, it also suggests that policies which increase the scope for human self-expression and risk-taking will reduce social frustration and increase well-being.

Looking Ahead

The world of textbook economics is perfect in itself, but importantly flawed as a tool of policy. As we have seen, it is static. It excludes precisely the things that make society flourish: people, institutions, culture. Yet its prestige and technical difficulty make it hard to question. However, the conventional approach is far from being a neutral tool of policy. On the contrary, it silently carries with it several damaging biases: towards centralisation in government; towards a flawed operational model for provision of public services; and against the natural human instinct to take risks. And finally, it constrains the very possibility of debate as to the kind of economic future we want to have, at precisely the moment we need that debate.

But all is not lost. There are other tools in the toolbox, other ideas we can consider. In particular, imperfect information opens the door to new ideas. If markets not only can but must operate on imperfect information, then we have no reason to think that the textbook model is perfectly efficient. But if that is true, then we have no reason to prefer only a maximally libertarian economy. The way is clear for a more nuanced debate as to what varieties of capitalism there are, and which of them we wish to move towards.

Specifically, we are looking for two things: an understanding of individual human beings which is not merely based on utility, and an economics which is new, dynamic and institutional. The rest of the book focuses on these, beginning with individuals.

4: The Danger of Happiness

If you're poor I hope you get rich
If you're rich I hope you get happy
Bob Dylan

We have seen, then, how British government is in the grip of an economic illusion. But it is not alone: over the past 40 years, the public understanding of human behaviour has increasingly reflected a standard view of man as perfectly rational, greedy and fearful, and hyper-sensitive to marginal gains and losses.

These two ideas are linked, and self-reinforcing. This standard economic view has become a default position, as we have seen. But it has also been propagated by many large organisations, including corporations and government itself. One valuable study has made this point by contrasting what it calls Theory X and Theory Y.

Theory X holds that people are shirkers, who will avoid work whenever possible. They are gullible and unambitious. They resist change, dislike responsibility and will only work if coerced towards an organisation's goals. Theory Y, by contrast, holds that people are naturally inclined to work, whether in their jobs or play. They are naturally enterprising, and willing to use their own ingenuity to solve problems. But that ingenuity is rarely tested in large organisations.

The point is that Theory X is self-fulfilling. If people are treated in a Theory X way, they become demoralised and unproductive. Those in charge then assume that this is how people really are—entrenching Theory X in their minds—and become still more controlling. This leads to more demoralisation, and so on. Controlling people thus worsens performance and service, generating more failure and more control. As people rise through these organisations, they become increasingly selected for, and wedded to, a Theory X view of the world.

But this economic view has not had it all its own way. On the contrary, there has also been a huge and growing literature of reaction. The countercultural cluster of views of the 1960s—that there is more to life than money, that economics can never do justice to the complexity and richness of human life and human experience, and that we should live for the day—is increasingly mainstream. It feeds into claims, charted by authors such as Oliver James, that materialism is creating an epidemic of depression as people find themselves aspiring to what they cannot achieve and unable to compete with their peers. It has been supplemented by growing fears about the impact of globalisation and turbulence in the global market economy. The result is conflict: we reject conventional economic thinking, but without quite knowing why. We yearn for an alternative, but we have nothing coherent to offer.

One result of this conflict has been the rise of "happiness theory", promoted in such recent best-sellers as *Happiness: Lessons from a New Science* by Richard Layard, a noted economist and former professor at the London School of Economics. Happiness theory is not simply the ancient idea that what really matters is happiness rather than, say, wealth or income. Rather, it claims that people's happiness can be measured; that happiness can be compared, managed and traded off as between different groups of people; that policy ideas should be assessed on the basis of its contribution to happiness; and indeed that the overall goal of public policy should be to maximise happiness.

At first glance it may look as though this emphasis on happiness is a counterblast to standard economics. After all, economic growth is not the be-all and end-all of human existence. And isn't the whole point of happiness theory to reject the caricature image of man as *Homo Economicus?*

In fact, however, happiness theory subtly reinforces the conventional picture: by simply substituting one set of human motivations for another, it leaves intact the broader framework of perfect markets, perfect information and perfect rationality that is so deeply problematic. Indeed it legitimises that framework. With obvious worries about human psychology partially addressed, it becomes yet harder for those that disagree to articulate their deeper concerns.

We can go further. This chapter will argue that Layard's happiness theory is, at least at present, a blind alley. Many people have argued against it on internal or external grounds. But the real point is that in one key respect it is fundamentally and dangerously misconceived. At its heart is exactly the kind of passive conception of the human self that we find in neoclassical economics.

But the story is not entirely bleak. For in contrast to this passive idea we can develop a positive, active and dynamic conception of the self, rooted in an ancient philosophical tradition dating back to Plato and the Ancient Greeks. It gives us a route from Theory X to Theory Y. Once we have this in hand, we can return much more fruitfully to our earlier questions about the status and nature of economics, and its role in public policy.

Layard and Happiness

To get to grips properly with the issues we really need a clear target to aim at, and a good place to start is with Professor Layard's book *Happiness*. Layard deserves great credit for focusing public attention on the issue, and on some of the causes, of unhappiness. His book has been both influential and controversial, and we cannot hope to do justice to it here. Nevertheless, a key part of the argument can be briefly summarised.

Layard is a follower of the English philosopher Jeremy Bentham, founder of utilitarianism, and with Bentham he believes that happiness is "hedonic" or based on pleasure. It is a state of mind, and so the goal of public policy is to maximise the pleasure experienced through this state of mind by the largest possible number of people.

Particular attention has focused on two claims. The first, reflecting a standard economic view of consumption, says that after a certain point greater wealth contributes diminishing marginal amounts of happiness. An extra £1,000 does not make the billionaire any happier, for example, but is usually a huge source of happiness to someone on the minimum wage. The second claim is that a person's happiness is a relative or positional matter: that it largely depends on changes in their status or position relative to their peers. On this view, it is of no relevance to Mr Smith's happiness how he fares compared to the Duke of Westminster. What matters to him is keeping up with the Joneses. Not only that: the desire for status forces people into a rat race. They work harder, but one person's relative gain is another's relative loss, so there is no net social benefit at all.

For Layard, these views have two specific effects: one on the taxation side, one on the spending side. The first is to create a moral case for high levels of taxation. On his view greater equality of income generates greater net happiness, because redistributing wealth confers happiness on the recipient at little cost to the (relatively well-off) person paying out. Moreover, he thinks higher taxes also counteract the rat race, by discouraging people from working harder. They thus contribute to a better work-life balance.

The second effect is to allow him to argue for huge public expenditure on addressing mental illness by such means as cognitive psychotherapy and the widescale provision of psychotherapeutic drugs. These treatments may be expensive. But the cost is, he estimates, vastly less than the happiness gains that relief from depression brings.

Layard's views have been much debated. Some commentators have questioned their factual basis, claiming that they are dependent on data which have been mispresented, and are undersupported by evidence. Others have argued that that they are internally inconsistent and methodologically flawed. Yet others have claimed that they are paternalistic, undemocratic and inhumane in their conclusions.

But the deepest problem is none of these. It is more philosophical: the whole argument is really a blind. It has been a truism since the time of Aristotle that the term "happiness" can cover many things. There is no single and stable concept in common use. Rather, the term has been used over the years in connection with a bewildering range of different ideas including well-being, self-fulfilment, blessedness, virtue, excellence, skill, moral or physical health, the full possession of one's faculties, wealth or property, honour, virtue and cultivated tastes, to name only a few.

But what about pleasure? Following Bentham, Layard identifies happiness with pleasure, and this allows him to use what people report about their feelings of pleasure as evidence for his theory. However, in so doing he crucially assumes, as we have seen, that happiness is fundamentally a state of mind. But if this is true, if happiness is just a matter of how we feel, then it is easy to improve our national happiness immediately. All that is necessary is to put Prozac or some other mind-pleasing drug into our water-supplies. Of course to do so would be absurd: among other things it would be an outrageous in-fringement of personal liberty. Yet in his advocacy of government provision of psychotherapeutic drugs on a mass basis, Layard comes close to this very view. On his account, the opium of the people is opium.

What has gone wrong here? The key point is that nothing in the under-lying theory has really changed. Layard purports to reshape policy around a new and missing category and thereby to make it more reflective of and more relevant to actual human needs. In reality, however, what he does is to take one unclear and unspecifiable value, "utility", replace it with another, "happiness", and then draw dubious policy conclusions on that basis. The remainder of the standard picture remains, with all its hidden problems and flawed presuppositions intact. Indeed, as noted, it is tacitly reinforced and further enfranchised by the appearance of change, and by the new rhetoric of happiness.

After all, it is not as though happiness has been missing from economic thought over the past two centuries. On the contrary, some notion of happiness or other has been assumed by economic debate from the begin-ning. A key point of the theory of GDP over the years, for example, has been to develop a broadly well-understood and quantifiable proxy for na-tional happiness, well-being or benefit. It may or may not have succeeded —opinions vary on this question. But the world's macroeconomists are hardly smacking their heads post-Layard from a sudden realisation that their subject is really about happiness. For almost all of them, it has been about happiness or something similar all along.

The Passive Self

Thus the real significance of happiness theory lies in what it leaves untouched: a deeply passive conception of what a human being is. We noted earlier that in standard economics people are not flesh-and-blood human beings but "agents" whose behaviour can be mathematically specified and modelled. In fact, however, even this language overstates the case: within the theory they are not even in any interesting sense agents, or indeed individuals, at all. Instead they are vessels for "utility", or bearers of preferences. Layard's happiness theory perpetuates this view. Happiness is merely a state of mind, and people are passive recipients of happiness. They are empty dials, which only flicker into life when some temporary pleasure pulses through them.

This view of the self as passive is not merely embedded in our standard economics. On the contrary, it permeates our intellectual history, most notably in some empiricist traditions that see humans as mere recipients of sensory inputs or impressions from outside. (Yet it is interesting to note that the idea of man as purely self-interested was given an early and trenchant refutation by David Hume, close friend of Adam Smith and arguably the greatest empiricist philosopher of them all, in his *Enquiry Concerning the Principles of Morals*.)

And the idea of people as passive selves is also deeply rooted in contemporary British life. It lies behind what many see as an administrative culture which is increasingly dumbed-down and risk-averse, which sets our children low educational and moral standards, which undervalues achievement, and which too readily accepts the second-rate. That culture draws on a pap idea of marketing as feeding the lowest urges of the widest segment of the population. It is neurotically afraid of abstract ideas and diverse achievement. It caters for people, rather than challenging them.

So this assumption that people are fundamentally passive has disastrous effects. But what is the alternative? Is there—to put the matter at its most abstract—an alternative conception of the self, of what it is to be human, which can be used to guide public policy? And if so, what difference would it make to our politics and to our public culture?

To answer this question we need to pull together various ideas that at first glance may seem only distantly related to each other. We begin in the 4th Century BC, with Plato's dialogue *The Republic*. *The Republic* is often seen, not without reason, as a rather authoritarian work. But early on Plato uses an imagined conversation about the nature of justice between Socrates and his followers to develop a profoundly worthwhile and rather liberal idea. Socrates thinks that the just person is happier than the unjust one, and in arguing for this he talks about happiness as a kind of self-fulfilment, and in particular as a matter of what he calls "doing your own thing". His thought seems to be that everyone has a distinctive capability or function, and happiness is a matter of developing that capability to the utmost.

We can find something similar in Aristotle. In the *Nicomachean Ethics*, Aristotle focuses on the role of action and habit in engendering happiness. Man is a social animal, he believes: humans are innately gregarious beings, who are embedded in social relationships. Happiness is always the ultimate end-goal and result of action, he suggests; and indeed it is itself a kind of activity, one of living well. Again, there is a connection to virtue: the person who repeatedly acts well becomes virtuous, in Aristotle's view, as good actions settle over time into good habits.

We can catch a glimpse of a similar line of thought in Locke, writing two millennia later from what is in many ways the radically different perspective of a Christian philosopher in his *Second Treatise of Government*. For Locke humans are naturally free and autonomous beings, who have been given the Earth in common. But in that case, if the Earth is their common inheritance, how can they come to own private property at all?

Locke's answer is that they own their own labour, and it is what he calls the "mixing" of this labour with other objects that confers a right of ownership to those objects, and so gives rise to the institution of private property. Thus the farmer who cultivates open land thereby establishes rights of ownership over that land—but, it should be noted, only so much as he can directly cultivate. Hence this process of mixing labour has a natural end, and property rights have an intrinsically human scale.

Scholars have toiled long and hard to attack Locke's idea of "mixing one's labour" as unclear or obviously mistaken. What does it mean? Is labour the kind of thing that can be mixed with an object at all? What happens when all the "open land" is occupied? Isn't Locke's idea simply a charter for self-enrichment by the haves over the have-nots?

However, if we read the idea of mixing one's labour less literally, it starts to look not merely not wrong, but importantly right. In effect, Locke is suggesting humans have a natural drive to shape, and so to personalise, their environments. Not only that, but these actions can in turn ground even the most fundamental institutions, such as rights to property.

Capabilities and the Active Self

The idea of a human being as fundamentally a bundle of capabilities, or of humans as striving for self-expression through the exercise of those capabilities, is not restricted to one philosophical or political tradition, however. On the contrary, it is astonishingly widespread. We can find it throughout the Christian tradition, of course, for example in St Paul's Epistle to the Romans. But it also features prominently in Hinduism, in the idea of Atma-Jnana or self-realisation; in the writings of the existentialists and Nietzsche; and prominently in the *1844 Manuscripts* of Karl Marx. It is an idea which rises above racial, political or religious categories.

With this in mind, we can assemble the broad outline of a completely different conception of the human self, and so of human well-being, to the passive one described above. It has three distinct components, which link the ideas of action, self-fulfilment, and social institution.

First, on this view the human self is not static but a dynamic, active force. It is autonomous, imaginative and creative, and its needs and interests constantly change and develop over time. It has actual and potential capabilities that naturally seek an outlet for self-expression. Secondly, people are social beings. They are not merely gregarious; rather, they have an instinct to change and personalise what is around them, and to link with others. Thirdly, human actions over time create habits, and good habits become virtues; shared habits over time create practices; and practices that have developed over time become institutions.

Now at this point the reader may be rather sceptical about the idea of "doing your own thing", with its overtones of Timothy Leary, Sergeant Pepper and the Summer of Love. Isn't the problem precisely that everyone nowadays is always doing their own thing? Instead, don't we need more discipline, more deference to authority and a return to traditional values?

But in fact this is not a call for a more permissive society; or for more narcissism in government, something of which the UK is rarely in short supply. Properly understood, "doing your own thing" both frees and constrains our understanding of human self-fulfilment.

First of all, it invites people to ask themselves what they stand for; what they care about, what they want to become, and what they can achieve. In short, who they are. Secondly, it is both highly personalised and optimistic about human potential. How you do your own thing may well radically differ from how I do mine. Everyone has, or can develop, his or her own distinctive skills or goals or capabilities. Personal success becomes a matter of fulfilling one's potential, not simply of a status rat race against others. Thirdly, it is egalitarian and non-hierarchical: we each have our own capabilities, so you and I can always learn from each other. But we are equals. Because humans have such astonishing potential in so many different directions, there is no single metric—least of all IQ—on which different people can be comprehensively assessed.

This line of thought is massively incomplete, of course—in particular, nothing has been said as to whether or how different capabilities should or even could be valued for policy purposes. But it is not presumptuous to suggest that it offers the kernel of a far richer and more dynamic basis for public policy than the dismal assumptions presently on offer. This is brought out by its affinity with a well-worked out theory of capabilities developed over the past 30 years by the welfare economist and philosopher Amartya Sen.

Beginning in 1979, Sen has argued that public policy should seek to benefit not such things as a person's utility, or access to basic goods, or equality of outcome or opportunity, but rather their capabilities. For Sen, these capabilities are very wide-ranging. They include basic bodily functions such as resistance to disease, situational advantages such as access to good nourishment, as well as more advanced capabilities such as the ability to earn a living, or to manage one's life independently.

This is a very attractive approach. It is not excessively materialist. It is positive, indeed idealistic, about people. It is open-ended and pluralist in its idea of the good life and of human flourishing. It stresses the institutions, habits, practices and culture from which capabilities spring and to which they contribute. It recognises that human happiness is too varied to be precisely defined, but is a by-product of action, and especially of the drive to self-fulfilment. And it brings out, crucially, a two-way relationship between freedom and capability. Capabilities require a certain freedom to be exercised. But people must have an adequate range of basic capabilities in the first place if they are to exercise their freedoms at all. In Sen's hands, therefore, a theory of capabilities can be both progressive and oriented towards freedom.

The same is true in our own case. But the emphasis is rather different. Sen is fundamentally arguing with an eye to developing countries, and his feels like more of an aggregative, top-down approach to policy-making. Our whole perspective is far more individual and bottom-up. For us, the challenge is not merely to change how government sees us, the people. It is to change how we see ourselves.

The Science and Psychology of Compassion

The active self, the self as a bundle of capabilities, is naturally engaged with its environment and with others around it. If the passive self is, metaphorically, an atom cut off from others, then the active self has carbon bonds constantly seeking to link with others. It is other-regarding. But the deeper point is that only an active conception of the self allows for the possibility of compassion. Only an active self can act in a way that expresses fellow-feeling. The active self is thus the common prerequisite to both compassionate conservatism and compassionate economics.

On this view, then, people are naturally compassionate; their self-fulfilment involves the development and exercise of their capabilities; and the expression of these capabilities in action is something for which they can be held properly responsible.

These claims may seem wild. But in fact there is an increasing amount of scientific evidence for them. In particular, recent research by Jean Decety and others suggests that there is a neural basis for compassion or empathy in the human brain. Thus people who observe others in pain, especially their partners, seem to process this recognition in part through their own pain centres. People who consider the emotional reactions of others process this through their own emotional neural systems. By contrast, certain autistic, narcissistic and anti-social personality disorders manifest themselves in a lack of empathy, or may cause their victims even to fail to recognise others as people at all.

Overall, then, there is good reason to think that people are naturally compassionate. Moreover, there is increasing evidence that the exercise of compassion is deeply psychologically rewarding. Thus several studies suggest that people who regularly give money, time or support to others enjoy better physical and mental health, have lower levels of depression and suicide and have increased longevity, compared to those who do not. Those who donate to charity reported higher levels of happiness than others. People who volunteer have lower mortality rates, better bodily functioning and lower rates of depression later in life than those who do not volunteer, especially if they spend more than 100 hours per year in volunteering, and if it involves repeated personal contact in helping strangers.

And the exercise of compassion is ultimately one of the sources of society itself. To continue our earlier metaphor: if the active self is an atom with carbon bonds, then we can think of families as small molecules, other institutions as larger ones, and society itself as the largest molecule of all, the composite of which the others are all parts. It has no fixed shape—it can be of any shape depending on how its individuals and institutions link together. But on its shape and composition depend many if not all of its characteristics.

The Threat to Altruism?

But the fact that compassion is a natural human instinct does not mean it is safe from threat. Some experts have described many young people in Britain today as, in effect, "battery children". They live in increasingly small and crowded city housing stock, and very often flats. They have limited access to green space and to regular exercise, while TV and computer games dominate their free time. On average, they spend only half an hour a day in "purposeful outdoor activity". A quarter of all young people live in one-parent families. In two-parent families the parents now often both work, and are shorter of free time and more financially indebted than their predecessors at any time in history. Role models and familial experience in childcare are in increasingly short supply. More than one in five young people suffers from mental health problems, while rates of suicide and self-harm among the young continue to rise.

We can push the argument further. Recent neurological research suggests that the instinct to co-operate with others is mainly developed in the early teen years. Not only that, but our willingness to treat others fairly and in a trusting way is heavily affected by the environment in which we grow up: "high trust" environments encourage "high trust" behaviour, and "low trust" environments encourage "low trust" behaviour. Early-life experiences create chemical pathways in the brain that reinforce feelings of fair dealing with others, and set expectations of such fair dealing in return—or not. Moreover, as adults our behaviour is radically affected by the environment and incentives we face. In the most difficult situations, even perfectly healthy and well-adjusted people can find themselves taking part in, and indeed enthusiastic for, acts of cruelty and neglect.

The growing possibility is that for many young people today it may be psychologically difficult to experience feelings of altruism, and so of fraternity or compassion, at all. Lacking a strong sense of trust, they may find it hard to offer trust to others and so simply opt out, thus in turn reinforcing feelings of alienation and disaffection. What they need is to be treated as human beings, as valuable in themselves. Yet they are losing their connection with others, and with nature. They face a world from which the personal dimension, the human touch, has largely been removed.

The issue could hardly be more serious, concerning as it does the squandering of so much talent and potential, and thus the very possibility of many young people having a worthwhile place within British society. Its implications in a world of low-cost terrorism and of increasing gun and knife crime are also obvious. It suggests we may be approaching a kind of "social singularity" or tipping point, after which renewing British society becomes immeasurably harder.

So What?

But so what? Fine words, one might say, but this brief foray into philosophical ideas and psychological research is just an academic exercise. So maybe government hasn't got it quite right. But these are pettifogging distinctions, which no politician could be expected to consider or even remember. They really make no practical difference. Policy rolls on, after all.

You could not be more wrong. Moving to a capabilities approach, and to this dynamic conception of human possibility, completely changes how we should view policy, and indeed politics itself. The crucial point is that a deep belief in the capabilities of others is a prerequisite of greater trust in government, and in society as a whole. A politics of responsibility requires an active conception of the self. You cannot trust someone you despise, and our present system of government despises people—both the people who work in it and the people whom it is designed to serve. It uses the rhetoric of empowerment, but its view of people is so debased that the result is confusion and failure.

The first thing a capabilities approach changes is the role of government. At present, as we have seen, the machinery of British government is very top-down, centralised, micro-managerial and hostile to intelligent innovation. A capabilities agenda changes all this. Government becomes far more pluralist, and cautious about intervening in people's lives. It sets standards and rules, and enforces them—but then it trusts people to do their own thing. So it might, for example, make available funding in blocks rather than prescribing how it is to be spent. It might prefer grants of money to voluntary organisations rather than contracts. And it would certainly devolve power to independent institutions, and hold them periodically accountable for outcomes.

The move to capabilities also pushes public policy to be far more holistic. It can take decisions based on a rich conception of human good, and not only a pounds, shillings and pence justification. Freed from the requirement to regard people as merely economic agents, policymakers can look more at what is actually happening, and why. It becomes possible to explain why certain personal qualities matter whose value cannot be modelled economically: qualities like loyalty, energy, personal warmth and creativity. It becomes possible to see how certain social phenomena have a cultural and not merely an economic basis. It becomes possible to understand the causes and effects of social frustration as a cause of social failure, and the quest for social status as a result.

Take teenage pregnancy, for example. The conventional wisdom on the centre-right is that teenage pregnancy is an economic reaction to a benefits system that "rewards", and so encourages, very young mothers to have children by giving them increased benefits and priority access to social housing. In some cases this may well be true—but it is only a part of a wider explanation.

As anyone who has worked with teenage mothers will tell you, these pregnancies are often a reaction to lack of love, lack of status, or lack of a role in life. A teenage girl is a young woman at a very vulnerable stage of her life. As a mother, she would gain a role—and a role of some status, which demands the attention of others. Is it any wonder if, seeing this and even without experience or resources or family support, she ends up pregnant? The point is clear: many social phenomena cannot simply be understood through standard economic models. Social policy cannot simply be carried out by tweaking marginal economic incentives. It must range far more widely.

Finally, the move to a capabilities approach opens up and invigorates public debate. The very idea of a debate or conversation is based on respect, on each treating the other as a participant in a shared activity. The Blair government's attempt at a Big Conversation was fatuous because no-one genuinely believed it did or could ever have respect for those taking part. The present approach, by contrast, sees every person as a fizzing bundle of actual or potential capability. Its principle is that all are to be respected, all are equal at the table. It means a limit to deference—be that deference to people, to theory or simply to power as such—and the steady embracing of evidence, experience, common sense, practical skill and institutional wisdom across a variety of fields. It works with the grain of human beings, not against it. And it is for these reasons that a capabilities approach is profoundly conservative.

There is an interesting final parallel to be drawn between the present approach and that of the social theorist Julian LeGrand. LeGrand distinguishes between knaves and knights, and pawns and queens. Thus public policy can in theory treat people as purely self-interested knaves, or high-minded knights; and it can also see them as passive victims of circumstance (i.e. pawns), or as active shapers of their own destinies (i.e. queens). This enables a rough-and-ready taxonomy of economic philosophies: socialists believe people are knights but treat them like pawns, while liberals believe people are knaves and treat them like pawns. If the present argument is correct, the compassionate conservative instinct is to believe all people can be knights, and—if it can—to treat them like queens.

Secondary Schools: A Case Study
The capabilities approach is not simply a set of ideas. It is a viewpoint, which can structure how we look at all public policy. Let us close this chapter by looking at the difference it could make to our secondary schools.

This is an area in which present government policy systematically insults the abilities of teachers, staff and students alike. The national curriculum has expanded to fill the entire teaching time of most state schools. It specifies across a whole range of subjects what the teacher is to teach, lesson by lesson, week on week, month on month over the year. There is little flexibility or scope for initiative in the classroom, and an endless testing regime that distorts teaching priorities and pedestrianises the classroom experience. Little account is taken of the difference between good and bad teachers — it is virtually impossible to remove a bad teacher from their position. Such is the preoccupation with academic outcomes that other activities are relegated to the sidelines. Meanwhile the head is endlessly bombarded with paperwork from the Department of Children, Schools and Families and "guidance" from ancillary quangoes setting out new central priorities and initiatives. Running through the whole system is an ideology of government in which education is seen as a matter of skills provision for industry, and schools are regarded simply as buildings.

Little wonder, then, that those involved are so preoccupied with levels of funding, as though funding differentials were all that separated good schools from bad. Little wonder that so many good school heads only succeed by bucking the system, or that so many teachers suffer from poor morale. Little wonder that achievement remains stubbornly low in so many schools. Worst of all: little wonder that so many pupils, having spent so much time without doing much real learning at school, become disaffected with learning as such. A 2008 Ofsted report found that 45% of schools surveyed failed to give an adequate conceptual grasp of mathematics to pupils. The most recent OECD study found that British children start their education younger and have longer school days than most other developed countries. Yet among 29 countries, only Mexico, Turkey and Israel keep fewer children in school after the age of 16.

This dire state of affairs is the result of many hands. But it has been profoundly influenced by our standard model of economics and its associated pathologies of government. Every effort is made to control people from the centre. Vital but intangible values such as those of teaching morale, pride and public service are underplayed in favour of incentives designed to tweak behaviour. Trust is driven out of the system.

A capabilities approach changes all this. It would see education not merely as skills training or as necessary to meet national manpower needs, but as a way into life in all its diversity: as a matter of learning to be human. This implies a different notion of what a school is: not a collection of buildings but an institution, and not standardized but each different in its own way. It implies a belief that a comprehensive education should not simply be about open access and needs-blind admission, but should be comprehensive in its sense of human possibility. It implies a drastic scaling-back of the national curriculum, and public encouragement for outside activities such as sports, art, drama, public speaking and above all music, which allow young people to stretch themselves in different directions. And it seeks to enable the creation of new schools—be they publicly or privately funded, and in corporate, trust or co-operative form.

The same sense of human possibility applies to its treatment of teachers and heads. It would drastically reduce paperwork and "guidance". It would give heads far more flexibility and freedom of action, for example to set school spending priorities in consultation with teachers and parents. It would recognise value added across many dimensions, so that schools are properly celebrated which develop young people from even the most disadvantaged backgrounds. It would end the present obsession with public examinations. But it would retain enough periodic exams to track progress, however imperfectly, and it would allow new exam alternatives to emerge that are deliberately and publicly tougher than at present.

This approach is a very demanding one. It is demanding on those who work in schools, a minority of whom now may well be happy within the current system of command and control, and will therefore be nervous about new freedoms and new responsibility. It is demanding on government, which must alienate a significant amount of power according to a clear multi-year plan, and then resist attempts to force it to meddle anew. It is demanding on pupils, since the inevitable result of this approach will be that they are encouraged to aspire and to achieve more. And it is demanding on the public, since it requires a high degree of patience and tolerance from them during a process of change.

But notice that all that has really changed is a viewpoint. No policy as such has been adopted. Nothing has been said about the "Swedish model", about "pupil premiums" or about "supply side reform". The new viewpoint has implications for all of these policy ideas, of course. But the point is that a huge amount of positive reform can be achieved on the basis of common sense and a new perspective, before making what may inevitably be more ideological commitments.

We can use the idea of capability, then, to ground a different set of assumptions about human beings in public policy. Instead of the passive self of orthodox economic theories, we can substitute a positive idea of the active self. We can move from Theory X to Theory Y. But the counterpart of this is a radically different conception of what economics is, and so a different analysis of what the fundamental drivers are of economic prosperity. This is the subject of the next chapter.

5: The Social Foundations of Economic Prosperity

The great dialectic in our time is not, as anciently and by some still supposed, between capital and labour; it is between economic enterprise and the state.

In economics the majority is always wrong.
J. K. Galbraith

The Napoleonic Wars were won in 1688. Before the reader leaps to denounce this obvious error, let us acknowledge that Napoleon himself was finally defeated at Waterloo in 1815. Nevertheless, the basic cause of his defeat was the bloodless arrival of William III on the British throne 127 years earlier.

How so? During the 17th Century, it will be recalled, Great Britain experimented unsuccessfully with three different forms of government: by the monarch under the periods of personal rule of James I and, in particular, Charles I; by parliament, briefly after the Civil War; and by the army under Oliver Cromwell. The Restoration of the monarchy in 1660 created an increasingly uneasy truce between these forces. This truce was ridden out by Charles II, but ultimately resulted in the enforced exile of the Catholic James II and the arrival of the Protestant Stadtholder of the Netherlands as William III.

William's arrival was an event of enormous political and religious importance, of course. But it also had huge economic significance. Under the new constitutional order, sovereignty now lay not with the King as such, but with the "King-in-Parliament". The King was enabled to hold executive power, especially in matters of defence, but only as constrained by parliament. The effect of this was to discipline the public finances. Before 1688, British monarchs regularly needed revenue, both to fund their own courts and to fight wars. But they were reluctant to do so through taxation, since this meant calling a parliament, and parliaments inevitably sought new rights and privileges from the Crown.

Accordingly, hard-up monarchs had long raised funds by selling off Crown estates, by creating and selling the rights to artificial monopolies such as in tobacco, and by "forced loans" from nobles and London bankers. Each had serious drawbacks: selling off estates meant the Crown had a smaller and smaller revenue base, which merely compounded the original problem; artificial monopolies pushed prices up and inhibited trade; and forced loans were a form of gentlemanly extortion and were rarely repaid.

After 1688 all this changed. Because the new monarch had less power, he was more trustworthy. Parliament would not allow William to default, and so his promises to repay loans suddenly became credible. The result was that Crown indebtedness rose from £1 million in 1688 to almost £17 million in 1697. Interest rates fell to reflect the new security of the loans, from 14% in the early 1690s to 6-8% before 1700, and only 3% by the 1720s. Much of the new money was spent on the War of the Spanish Succession, in which the Duke of Marlborough won his great victories in the first decade of the new century.

William's arrival also released a huge wave of new ideas, including Dutch business practices and financial expertise. The first long term loan was made in 1693, and the Bank of England was founded in 1694. Credit was increasingly available for adventurous British entrepreneurs and traders, and a world of commercial opportunities lay before them. The result was to make Britain by far the most prosperous and successful nation in the world for almost two hundred years.

France had long been the one great continental superpower under Louis XIV. But her autocratic and personal monarchy, rigid and centralised administration and inert parliament created a weak system of government. She lacked the flexibility, trust and free institutions to generate a large entrepreneur class and above all, she lacked credit. The government defaulted repeatedly on its debts. When the Napoleonic Wars came to be fought, Britain had enjoyed interest rates 4-7% below French rates for decades. It had used its astonishing access to capital to re-equip and copper-bottom the Royal Navy, among other things, and sea power was to prove a crucial factor in the struggle against Napoleon. Indeed, the Navy was able to sustain a policy of having more fighting vessels than the rest of the world combined for most of the 19th Century. Thus did a constitutional change in 1688 underwrite military success in 1815.

Introducing I-C-E

This brief venture into history is a huge cautionary tale. It perfectly illustrates the long-term dangers of our present system of government writ large. France failed in the 18th Century because it was subject to a centralised, autocratic and personal government, which was not constrained by parliament or disciplined by competing sources of power. Britain succeeded because it was flexible, free and enterprising, massively open to new ideas, and possessed of a balanced constitution and a well-grounded rule of law.

These are precisely the foundations of economic success today. We can think of them under the headings I-C-E: Institutions, Competition and Entrepreneurship. Each of these can of course be understood in a standard textbook way, as we have noted. But we will look at them rather differently.

However, it is important to note up-front that these economic foundations were and are as much social as economic. By the early 19th Century Britain had not merely the strongest economy, but in many ways the strongest society of any major European state. Per capita income was by far the highest in Europe. Poverty was in general far less widespread and less deep than elsewhere. British levels of literacy and numeracy dwarfed those of France and the continent. And these social strengths were vital to her success, in warfare as in business.

Needless to say, the point is not that we should abolish the welfare state and return to the Poor Laws. Nor is it that a free economy and a free society always go together; they need not, at least in the short run. But the two are inseparably joined in Britain. We have learned the lesson that all economic policy has social implications. We now need to relearn the converse lesson: all social policy has economic implications. The foundations of our economic prosperity are social foundations. Thus the way to a stronger economy in Britain lies in part through a quite different approach to social policy.

Institutions

Readers of *Compassionate Conservatism* will recall the absolutely fundamental role which independent institutions play within this political
viewpoint. Constitutionally, they promote good order, restrain excessive
power and protect the basic freedoms of the citizen. But they also give
shape and meaning to our lives: they command our loyalty and affec-
tion, and they help define us and shape our identity. Finally, they are
the repositories of much human wisdom and knowledge, embodying the
collective experience of previous generations, experience which can and
frequently does outstrip the wisdom of those who would reform them.

The significance of this line of thought is that in place of a simple op-
position between the individual and the state, it substitutes a three-way
relationship between individuals, institutions and the state. It is when this
relationship is functioning well that societies flourish. This requires each
element in the triangle to be active and energised in its own right. But
when it is, then each imposes a constraint and a discipline on the other
two. It holds them more accountable. It forces them to do more, to converse with each other, and the whole becomes stronger.

Economically, we can think of institutions as all settled arrangements, formal and informal, which facilitate the exchange of goods
and services. They can be utterly abstract or very concrete: they can
be rules, customs, traditions, and practices, or they can be fish markets
and car boot sales. They can be specifically instituted by private or
public action, or they can simply arise. They can be IBM, or they can
be money. The economic importance of institutions such as a trusted
common currency, readily available credit, secure property rights, and
an established and enforceable law of contract has long been known.
But as we have already noted, the importance of intangible norms and
conventions may be no less great.

The effect of adopting an institutional perspective is to recreate many
of the elements of economic thinking that are purged by the conventional approach. The world of conventional economics is arid, impersonal
and atemporal. The institutional world, however, is fantastically diverse,
richly peopled and heavily influenced by the past. It restores, indeed it
has built into it, a presumption against one-size-fits-all thinking. And it

places a higher burden on government to justify state action, which must inevitably disrupt existing institutions and shared knowledge.

Competition

Economic institutions and individuals often co-operate with each other. But they also compete. Indeed, it seems to be a deep part of human nature or human culture to do both.

Some people regard competition and markets as intrinsically bad, in the belief that they put people into rivalry with each other and feed off and so encourage emotions of greed and fear. As we have noted, there is certainly a problem when a narrowly economic conception of human good and human values leaches back into society as such. And there is a further problem when policymakers, under the influence of standard rigor mortis economics, forget that markets are culturally created and sustained and adopt a purely laissez-faire approach.

But as an economic matter, it should not need saying that competition and markets are absolutely vital to society's well-being. This is not just because of their role in resource allocation and wealth generation. On the contrary, well-functioning markets are the greatest tool of economic development ever created. Competitive prices tend to be low prices, which help the poor and the economically unwary, and markets have made a huge difference to many of the poorest nations on Earth. And finally, markets are tools of communication and exchange, which put people in touch with each other who may otherwise have no affinity—religious, social or ethnic—with each other at all. They are in this sense a source, not of social breakdown, but of social cohesion.

On the deeper issues, however, we again need a shift in perspective. Recall that in the conventional economic world, competition is understood as a state. "Perfect competition" is a virtual state of affairs in which everything—prices, quantities, products—is settled and fixed. There is no change, so there is no scope for discovery or learning. Most importantly, by thinking of people as mere economic agents, this approach treats them simply as passive recipients and not as dynamic forces for change.

When government economists and politicians adopt this static view, the effect is to inhibit them from seeing markets as evolving processes which change over time. The question becomes not "Can we really understand what is going on here?" and automatically leaps to "How can this state of affairs be improved?" or "What can government do to help?" And so the door is opened to all kinds of ill-advised state intervention and tinkering.

But this is wrong-headed. Competition is not static but dynamic. It can be cut-throat or moderate, and it can wax or wane. Markets are evolutionary, transient and sometimes semi-chaotic. Generally unpredictable, they are often driven by fashion or group-think. And not all markets are the same. Some are deep, resilient and slow to change, while others are shallow, jumpy and apt to clog up easily. Sometimes the same markets change their basic character over time, depending on who is active in them. Just look at the world's financial markets in 2007-8.

Again, then, one-size-fits-all solutions are bound to fail. Consider our schools once more. Any good teacher knows that children naturally both compete and co-operate. The idea that competition can somehow be eliminated from schools by government fiat is simple nonsense. And it is also profoundly misguided, since competition is a means, one among many, to encourage people of any age to improve their capabilities, and far too many young people leave school today with little to show for their time there.

But competition has limits. You can have competition for which a child is not ready—competition which is too narrow or too intense. There are many areas of human capability and attainment, and so of school life, where competition is hardly relevant at all. And different schools have different values and characters. In other words, competition in schools is inevitable, dynamic and manageable. How to manage it, is a judgement call. Only good heads and good teachers—and certainly not government—can make that call successfully.

The rejection of one-size-fits-all solutions cuts both ways, however. It can also apply to libertarians such as those who adopt the one-size view that more choice is always good. Take the market for baked beans. It does not take the average student long to trawl down a supermarket shelf in the first week of term and figure out what the different baked bean options are, how much they cost, and what extra value he gets from larger packs or buying own-brand. He can, if he wishes, buy beans every week for a term or a year. In this case wide choice is good. It is hard to imagine a decent case for further regulation.

But what about the markets for mortgages or car insurance? These are rare or one-off purchases, in which people systematically mistake what is in their financial best interest. Mistakes are typically very expensive. And the decisions involved can be fantastically complex and hard to optimise. Indeed, some of the main suppliers may gain from the complexity, if purchasers are unwilling or unable to shop around endlessly. Here the case for regulation to simplify and standardise the different alternatives in the market—and so restrict choice—is much stronger. People are not economic androids, after all.

The point is that too much choice can itself inhibit good decision-making. Pensions and other retirement plans are almost always financially good for you due to tax breaks and other subsidies. But a recent study of 800,000 employees in America showed that the larger the number of retirement plans they were offered, the less likely it was that they would join any plan at all. In some countries, too, the government itself is forcing people to make private decisions about savings or healthcare. In cases like these, it can make good sense—it can enable human freedom rather than restricting it—to have a smaller number of basic choices, plus an opt-out for those who regard themselves as genuine experts.

Entrepreneurship

The last of our three foundations is entrepreneurship. The normal picture of an entrepreneur might be of an Alan Sugar or an Anita Roddick; that is, a successful businessman or woman who has made millions from a brilliant idea. On this view, entrepreneurs are unusually bright, or driven, or nervy. They go to business school or have science PhDs. Capitalism is about capital, and the reason why it needs entrepreneurs is because they create the capital.

Within our received economic theory, however, entrepreneurs do not exist as such at all. Not only that: they cannot exist. All markets are deemed to be in equilibrium, so there are no free lunches and no unexploited opportunities. For the same reason, there can be no competition, and prices never move. In this world, don't forget, nothing ever happens.

The standard view thus makes it all but impossible for government to understand entrepreneurs and entrepreneurship. Entrepreneurship is a necessary, vital, chaotic, unpredictable and creative process. And as such it is a process that is generally beyond state control, however much this and other governments talk about it and try to foster it. Typically government ignores or misconceives the negative impact of new policy initiatives on existing businesses; as with Sure Start, which greatly undermined the provision of private nursery school places in the UK. Or it grossly overestimates the effect of new spending on entrepreneurial activity; as with the Treasury's many ineffective attempts to improve private sector productivity and rates of innovation. Or it funds some oxymoronic attempt at state entrepreneurship directly.

Yet the conventional view of an entrepreneur is not quite right either. Entrepreneurs are not always unusually bright or driven. If they were, there would be a lot fewer of them and Great Britain would be a lot poorer than it is. A better way to think of entrepreneurship is as a kind of alertness to opportunity. On this view, entrepreneurship is 90% the discovery of a hidden saving. The entrepreneur might be the inventor of the mobile phone. It might be the Indian importer of silks to the UK. But it might also be the housewife who stretches a limited budget further by walking down to CostCo for her bulk purchases.

Such a wide definition might seem meaningless. But the point is precisely that entrepreneurship is everywhere. It is not a business activity so much as one aspect of the ceaselessly interesting and creative nature of human beings. And it implies that, far from always being in equilibrium, markets are hardly ever in any kind of meaningful equilibrium. Writers, for example, used quills until the late 19th Century. Since then they have used fountain pen, the typewriter, the electric typewriter, the dot-matrix printer, the inkjet printer, the laser printer and the colour laser printer. In other words, the market kept on changing as alert entrepreneurs noticed what hidden costs and unsatisfied needs were out there and how they could be dealt with. Who knows what will come next?

On this view, too, there is nothing about entrepreneurship that requires entrepreneurs to have capital of their own. Rather, what matters is imagination—the ability to spot or conceive opportunities—and a willingness to take risks. If the opportunity is good enough, then the capital will normally be available. Indeed, the possession of capital of one's own may and often does reduce entrepreneurship, by reducing the appetite for risk.

The significance of the I-C-E perspective here is thus threefold. First, it is egalitarian. Successful business entrepreneurs rightly deserve to be honoured for their role in wealth creation. But entrepreneurs are not a special class, and market processes are not intrinsically biased towards the haves over the have-nots. There are no particular barriers of knowledge or wealth or background that prevent us all from being highly entrepreneurial if we choose, and it is this wider energy that underwrites our prosperity.

Secondly, I-C-E reminds us that entrepreneurship is not just about business. It is embedded in society, and some of the greatest entrepreneurship in the UK is to be found in not-for-profit organisations, and in co-operatives—all the more so since they generally have limited capital reserves.

And finally, it highlights the limits of government intervention yet again. Indeed, it suggests that an educational culture which is slanted towards business and other strictly "relevant" subjects may be blinkered and misconceived. The idea of entrepreneurship as a kind of alertness implies that what we need from our schools are not pre-packaged little business-people or workers as such, but generalists with open, inquiring and wide-ranging minds. Now that's a revolutionary thought.

The I-C-E perspective thus takes things we think we already understand, like competition and entrepreneurship, and looks at them in a new and rather different way. It is highly unorthodox. Indeed, it is sceptical about the very idea of orthodoxy. As a result, it can encourage us to look more carefully at some apparently obvious and standard ideas.

Compassionate Economics

Taking the last two chapters together, then, we can see that Compassionate Economics has two sides to it. The first is a distinct conception of what a human being is, as what we have called an "active self" with huge actual or potential capabilities. The second is the view that the foundations of economic prosperity are social foundations: independent institutions, the right balance of competition and co-operation, and widespread entrepreneurship. There is a marked contrast between this dynamic and creative perspective and the static sterility of our orthodox economics.

Recall that as a political viewpoint, Compassionate Conservatism stressed independent institutions and horizontal human ties, the conversation of many equal voices over the command of one voice, the wisdom of crowds over the fallibility of central control. The idea of compassion here is one of fellow-feeling, not of pity: one of identification, concern and sympathy with others, not one of condescension to them. Its emphasis is not on what the state can do for you, or you for the state, but on what we can do for each other. It is a philosophically coherent and well-founded viewpoint, not merely an adventitious group of ideas or a laundry list of policies.

Compassionate Economics reflects and extends these deeper commitments. In the first place, it rejects any monopoly of ideas—and so it has no truck with the present monopoly of textbook economics within British government. It opens the doors to new wisdom both within the discipline and outside, and it places a great responsibility on those in government to become wiser as to the limits of their thinking. We have seen some recent interest in behavioural economics, through discussion of books such as *Nudge* and *Predictably Irrational*. Compassionate Economics consolidates and extends this train of thought, and blends it with insights from other more neglected areas of economics, and from other disciplines such as history and philosophy.

Secondly, Compassionate Economics does not privilege economics as such, but recognises it as one language, one partial and limited way of representing the world, among many. It recognises what unreliable guides even the greatest economists may be when they cease to describe, and start to advise and predict. It understands that often the greatest power of a mathematical model is rhetorical: as a means to recruit others to a predetermined view. It rejects the increasingly accepted hierarchy in which economics trumps politics—as though the ability to point to a detailed cost-benefit analysis or statistical regression automatically exhausted political debate. It detests jargon and unwarranted deference. It is sceptical of consultants and advisers who enjoy many of the privileges of power without its responsibilities. It prefers open debate, plain words and common sense.

Thirdly, Compassionate Economics is generous in its view of people. It sees people not merely as economic agents, but as human beings: as fizzing bundles of capability and potential. It rejects the idea that economics itself is a purely sterile and formal discipline. It seeks to break the loop in which government treats people like cattle, reinforces social demoralisation—and is then somehow surprised when people opt out or object. It is naturally predisposed to human freedom.

Left-Wing, Right-Wing or What?

Politically, what emerges is both new and distinctive. As we have seen in some detail, Compassionate Economics calls into question not merely key policies, but the most basic policy assumptions, of the present government. Not merely as misguided, but as utterly misconceived. But it also offers a clear critique of some of the keynote policies and assumptions of the Thatcher government.

By contrast, the present viewpoint is less radical and more conservative. It is unabashedly pro-market, but sees markets differently to the present conventional view of them. It is neither controlling nor simply laissez-faire. Its emphasis on Institutions, Competition and Entrepreneurship is founded not on a purely economic conception of human good, or on "happiness", but on a profound and well-considered respect for individuals and for human capabilities. It is principled, but not rigidly so. Rather, it is pragmatic and non-ideological in character; a matter of instinct and judgement rather than the automatically consistent application of a political doctrine.

The effect of this is that, while evidently conservative, Compassionate Economics cannot easily be described with the established political categories of Left and Right. But this also gives it more freedom to innovate, sometimes very vigorously, and more freedom to act in accordance with simple common sense. Rules are necessary for effective government – but so are simplicity and a measure of discretion. Giving consumers more choice is often a good idea – but not always. Private ownership is the heart of capitalism – but sometimes private companies are not the best means to deliver a public service. What results is a politics of doubt, not of faith – of judgement, not of ideology.

In part for this reason, Compassionate Economics seems to capture and unify many apparently disparate threads of thought now within the centre-right. It gives deep intellectual support to the centre-right's critique of the Government and instinct for pluralism, diversity and decentralisation. It accords very well with current concerns to understand and strengthen the family. But it also fits well with the stress now being laid on strengthening the institutions of government, including a more powerful and independent-minded Parliament and new measures to safeguard monetary and, increasingly, fiscal policy from overly political interference. It explicitly embraces good public services, as a means to empower people, but implies a radical reshaping in the way those services are delivered. Indeed, it suggests that there are enormous gains in efficiency and the prevention of waste to be had from a more intelligent approach to delivering public services.

Two Worries

At this point, however, the reader may be feeling rather perplexed. Where are the usual soundbites? What's happened to tax cuts, fiscal policy, the rolling back of state, or any of the other supposed staples of centre-right thinking on economics? What does Compassionate Economics have to say about monetary policy and interest rates? The discussion so far doesn't feel like it has had anything much to do with economic policy at all.

This is as it should be. This book is not about economic policy as such, or even new economic ideas. It is about how we understand the fundamental drivers of our prosperity. Its goal is to question our basic assumptions about economics, and to forge a new and distinctively compassionate conservative viewpoint from which the whole spectrum of policy—economic and other—can be addressed. Any well-considered viewpoint naturally generates new ideas. And as we shall see in the final chapter, Compassionate Economics is extremely radical and fertile in its policy implications.

But this in turn generates a further worry. It's all very well to criticise our conventional economics, one might think. But that economics is massively widely studied in our universities, it is a well-organised and well-understood body of theory, and it is supported by a large amount of empirical work. Where is the intellectual backing for all this I–C–E guff?

This criticism misses the target. There is a wide gulf between the economics that is practised in British government today, and the frontiers of the subject in academia. Academic economists are only too aware of this, and of the limitations of their discipline, as we have noted. They are aware of the profound difference between the descriptive study of economics and the norm-based practice of recommending and implementing changes to policy on the ground. And they are aware of the rather poor record of academic economists in making useful economic predictions.

The real problem lies not within the academy, as we have seen, but in how economics is (mis)understood within politics, within public administration and within society. We need to break the present stale monopoly, open up public debate to new ways of thinking, and give policymakers new scope and new licence to think creatively about possible solutions. That opening-up of debate is far more important than any particular contribution to the debate itself.

In fact, however, the I–C–E perspective does not lack intellectual rigour. In technical terms, it is a blend of institutional, behavioural and "Austrian" economics. Each of these has its own history, its own body of academic research and ideas, and its own respected proponents.

Nor does the present approach lack evidence. On the contrary, it is supported by a large and increasing body of academic research. It helps to explain Britain's historic prosperity, as we have already seen. And it can also go some way to explain more recent events. The relative fortunes of Germany and the UK since the Second World War, for example, have been closely geared to how much each has placed on maintaining free and independent institutions, orderly markets and conditions of economic freedom in which individual entrepreneurship can succeed.

The fall of communism in Eastern Europe and Russia can also be understood in these terms. In effect these countries suffered a triple failure: virtually no free and independent institutions, hardly any genuine competition and little (legal) entrepreneurship. The countries that have flourished since 1989 have been those in which these three elements have been re-established and re-grounded in existing traditions and folk memories. And the record of Western technical advisers in assisting the transition from Communism to capitalism has been an extremely mixed one, precisely because they have often promoted a foolish economic orthodoxy that ignored local circumstances and these fundamental drivers of prosperity alike.

So far, then, we have a vision. What we now need is policy. This is the subject of the next chapter.

6: Compassionate Economics

The power of jazz is that a group of people can come together and create art, improvised art, and can negotiate their agendas with each other ... and that negotiation **is** *the art.*
Wynton Marsalis

Polish society used to be an aquarium. Communism turned it into fish soup. The challenge is to turn it back into an aquarium again.
Polish saying, 1989

We have grown up with a caricature of economics. But it is an influential caricature, and it has had two specific effects. The first is political: to ratify and encourage a 30 year trend towards centralisation, micro-management and faulty policy-making in government. The second is social: to promote a debased and narrow view of human beings as merely greedy and fearful profit-maximisers. Both these tendencies are self-reinforcing.

According to the old textbooks, the financial crash of 2008 could never have occurred. Aware of the potential risks, people would not have borrowed so much, banks would not have lent so much, the regulatory system would have been barely tested and the interbank and money markets would have continued to function without government support. Yet that colossal crash did in fact take place, markets seized up, many famous banks ceased to exist, the powers of government to manage economic disorder were stretched to breaking point, and the human consequences are likely to be dire. As Martin Wolf noted in the *Financial Times*, every important safeguard failed. No greater proof is needed of the limits of man's economic rationality. Thus we need to rethink the fundamentals from the bottom up.

Lessons of the Crash

But what difference would an I-C-E perspective have made? In the first place, it would have made all involved—politicians, regulators and bank executives—far more aware of how hard humans find it to assess risk, and of the well-known human predilection to prefer a benefit now, and to discount or ignore future costs. Secondly, it would not have allowed those politicians, regulators and executives automatically to assume that markets can efficiently assess the creditworthiness either of individuals or banks. Thirdly, it would have been clear from the outset as to the importance of the Bank of England standing as lender of last resort, a role which is inexplicable on the standard economic model, in which prices are always efficient and liquidations are already priced in and so do not affect markets. And fourthly, it would have had a far more realistic conception of the value of competition within financial services: as a means to greater efficiency and better allocation of resources, and not simply as a good in itself. The result would have been a far more sceptical and realistic attitude to the various booms already described.

Above all, I-C-E would have made us all far more sensitive to the dangers posed by the changing nature and increasing size of financial institutions. The old financial order had many weaknesses, but crucially, its institutions had clearly defined roles. The commercial banks and building societies had capital from depositors and investors, but took as little risk as possible. The brokers and merchant bankers were advisers and agents. They acted on behalf of investors and corporate borrowers, who took the risk and made the returns or losses.

The beauty of the whole lay in the different and interlocking roles of the various players, and the minimisation of conflicts of interest. And this was helped by the different institutional forms involved. The banks were companies, because they needed shareholder capital to sustain their balance sheets. The building societies were mutuals, because the mutual form facilitated the extension of credit to the less well-off. The brokers and merchant bankers were partnerships, because they did not need much capital and knew that their partners would guard their own funds far more zealously than those of any outside shareholders.

But look now at the financial markets, and what do we see? The original roles of these institutions have been submerged in a huge wave of capital. Conflicts of interest have become massive and endemic. Partnerships have disbanded. Building societies have demutualised. And thus the pluralism and diversity of their institutional forms have been replaced by one monopoly form: that of the shareholder corporation. Our financial markets have been damagingly corporatised.

With this corporatisation has come three things. First, there has been a deep and damaging separation of risk and reward. When the markets go up, the bankers do well. When they go down, the shareholders—and ultimately British taxpayers—suffer. This creates a structural incentive for banks to take more risk than capitalism, which is based on private property and the value of active ownership, should properly allow. Secondly, there are now no natural limitations on the size of financial institutions. As the fallout of the Lehman Brothers bankruptcy showed, an increasingly large number of financial institutions cannot be allowed by government to fail—yet it is barely within the power of government to save them. And thirdly, the financial services sector has increasingly been seen simply as an industry like any other, rather than as providing the fundamental plumbing on which the global economy relies.

From a policy perspective, the crash has revealed a gigantic failure of governance: within financial institutions, within the regulators and within government itself. As many commentators have noted, the banks competed furiously with each other to grow their mortgage books with poorer and poorer credits. The Government took the badly motivated and foolish decision in 1997 to remove banking supervision from the Bank of England, an issue over which then-Governor Eddie George almost resigned. There was a huge consequent loss of supervisory experience and expertise, and a damaging dispersion of regulatory responsibility under the so-called tripartite system. Both the Government and the regulators have been far too complacent over the past decade in the face of escalating warning signs, in a sector that over-dominates the British economy. The Government has itself hugely over-borrowed at the top of the market. And the lack of cash savings as people borrowed to invest in property has made them doubly vulnerable to the present downturn.

Rebuilding the Foundations

Some, perhaps many, of these problems could have been avoided if the Government had given up its preoccupation with 1970s textbook economics and adopted a different perspective. But the most fundamental issues are the ones we started with: what kind of capitalism do we want? And how can we rebuild the foundations of our future prosperity?

These issues are so large that they far outstrip the scope of this short book. And they stretch still further if we take seriously the notion of capabilities sketched in Chapter 4. We have already seen the profound difference which a focus on human capability would make in secondary education. But now think what it would mean to import a capability agenda fully into policy on the arts, culture and sports. These areas have long been treated as lesser priorities by government, although the National Lottery has in many ways been a brilliant institutional innovation. But a government that saw human capability at the heart of social and economic regeneration would surely place huge emphasis here. After all, one of the key messages of this book is that good social policy and a strong society are fundamental to a strong economy.

However, rather than run the whole gamut of policy now, let's look at three specifically economic areas where Compassionate Economics could directly improve our future prosperity: in the private sector, in the public sector, and straddling the two. In each case we find the same pattern: over-adherence to conventional economics leading to suboptimal outcomes, which the present perspective can potentially improve.

Private Sector

We have already noted how financial institutions have increasingly become shareholder corporations. Perhaps this should not be surprising, for the corporation (or company) is by far the most influential economic institution in the world today. Well over 90% of all non-governmental economic activity is conducted through corporations. Our media are saturated with the brands, imagery and values of corporations. We live in a world of corporate capitalism. And these corporations are not functioning as well as they should do.

The issue is not so much that of corporate responsibility, important though that is. It is one of ownership and accountability. Pooling resources in corporate form allows people to do more and to share risk. Corporations were originally enabled by specific grant of the sovereign to encourage risk-taking and the creation of capital. And in due course they came to enjoy limited legal liability. Why? Because it was widely recognised that corporate activity served the public good, and it was widely believed that corporate power would be limited to actions consistent with the public good. Thus a whole nation could benefit from the fruits of exploration, innovation and trade.

But today many of our largest public companies resemble bad governments in their levels of risk aversion and bureaucracy. They may have the outward forms of good governance but the reality is that their managements are often complacent and unaccountable, while auditors, remuneration consultants and corporate pension fund trustees are insufficiently independent. These firms are too focused on the short-term, and too much of their revenue is used up in executive compensation. Twenty years ago the average chief executive of a FTSE 100 company earned 17 times the average employee's pay; now it is more than 75 times.

We have had many useful reports and governance codes over the years. But the real point is that there is still a huge vacuum of ownership. These firms have investors who regard investments as betting slips, not owners who regard them as property. All parties have in effect swallowed the standard economic view, on which managers and directors are merely agents of the shareholders, corporations are merely bundles of contractual relationships, and there is no sense apart from the effects of the invisible hand in which corporations exist to serve the public good. And they have used that view to rationalise inactivity, by pointing out (correctly) that there is often a "free rider" problem in which an active owner bears 100% of the costs but only part of the benefits of their ownership. And so corporate value is lost, often until the point where the company is bought by venture capital funds with a small number of very active owners who can then take the steps necessary to rebuild it.

But here again the standard view is both partial and inaccurate. The directors of a corporation are legal fiduciaries, not merely economic agents. The shareholders are owners, not merely investors. The original institutional context, which linked appropriate corporate power to public wellbeing, is largely missing. To talk solely of risk and reward is to ignore the crucial dimension of active ownership, on which healthy capitalism depends. The result is to destroy value and entrench underachievement.

This is not a rant against Anglo-American capitalism or the need to reward talented people: quite the opposite. But the evidence across the UK and US is fairly clear. Many reputable studies have been carried out looking for a significant and sustained correlation between senior executive compensation and long-term corporate performance: none—none—has been found. Instead, there is a close correlation between executive pay and size of company, creating a strong incentive towards increased takeover and merger activity. Takeovers always benefit senior managements, win or lose. But in fact 60% of them destroy economic value.

By contrast, well-owned companies deliver better long-term performance, and are recognised as doing so. A 2002 McKinsey study which looked at 200 top global investors found that three-quarters of them would pay a premium for companies with good governance. Two other studies, from ISS and Deutsche Bank, have found that good governance improves profitability and lessens risk in US and UK companies respectively.

What, then, can government do? The key is to promote the exercise of independent ownership: by institutional shareholders, by corporate directors, and by trustees in corporate pension funds. Here are four simple suggestions for how to do so. The first is vigorously to enforce the trust law of ownership on financial institutions. A share's vote is part of its value, and the trustees or directors of investment trusts, pension and hedge funds and other investing institutions should be made clearly legally accountable for its proper exercise. The second is to make it easier for shareholders to nominate entirely independent non-executive directors of their own choosing to corporate boards. This would create an independent link between the shareholders and the board, and break many currently cosy arrangements whereby non-executive directors are too close to the chief executive.

Our third suggestion is for non-executive directors alone to choose remuneration consultants and auditors, via the relevant board committees. Again, this would introduce greater accountability and transparency, especially on the ratchet on pay that comes from benchmarking senior executive compensation. And the fourth is for pension fund trustees, many of who are also corporate employees, to be explicitly required to act solely in the long-term interests of their beneficiaries, and to be protected in law when they do so. This would limit the power of boards to control corporate pension funds, and help to make them more genuinely independent financial institutions.

These are four simple proposals, which would help to reintroduce active ownership into our corporations, banks and financial institutions. But their effect is potentially enormous. Making more companies work slightly harder through better ownership would have a gigantic effect on Britain's competitiveness and prosperity as a nation. It would lift profitability, employment and pay scales, while restraining remuneration in the boardroom. And even a small improvement in shareholder returns would massively strengthen the country's pension system over the long term.

Public Services

We can apply the same broad approach to British public services. These have changed over the past 50 years in four broad phases: expansion in the 1940s and 1950s, stasis in the 1960s and 1970s, selective retrenchment in the 1980s, and further extension after 1997. During this period government has tried many different structures and approaches to the provision of services, repeatedly confronting the basic truth that state control tends to inefficiency while completely free markets can lead to unfair outcomes.

In Chapter 2 we noted how conventional economic thinking had reinforced a tendency in government to centralisation and top-down control of people through the tax and benefits system. That thinking ignored independent private and third sector institutions. And it wrongly treated people as economically rational in the standard sense. On the one hand, they were expected to be able to understand and cope with the fantastic complexities of the tax credits system, of pension credits and other benefits. On the other, these systems ignored the systematic ways in which people do in fact misjudge risk, assess uncertainty and deal with loss.

Again, we need to ask what difference Compassionate Economics could make here. There are many, but here are three large ones. First, and not surprisingly, it would imply a significant reshaping of public services to reflect how people actually think and behave. This would mean, for example, taking many of the least well-off people out of the tax system altogether, rather than submit them to the complexities and unanticipated losses of the Tax Credits system. It would mean a reduction in pensions means-testing and a huge simplification of Pension Credits. And it would mean an extension into other areas of health and social care of Direct Payments and Individual Budgets, which allow many disabled people more autonomy and control over their lives.

The second difference lies in the support Compassionate Economics gives to public service commissioning. Public service commissioning seeks to balance the respective roles of the state and the market. Accordingly, on this approach the state sets broad outcomes and financial parameters to achieve certain agreed social goals, and then invites tenders from different organisations to achieve those goals.

Take Incapacity Benefit, for example, where debate has been polarised for too long between acquiesence in welfare dependency and attacks on scrounging. As all the main political parties now recognise, there is clearly a huge opportunity here for the state to commission private and independent sector organisations to retrain and move many of the current 2.7 million people on IB back into jobs, and to make sure they are able to keep those jobs. And there is similarly huge scope for the state in education to allow not-for-profit organisations to set up schools and be paid an agreed rate per pupil by the state. If this approach were combined with a top-up payment for poorer pupils, it would target the most deprived communities and so be highly socially progressive.

These examples show how the welfare state can be reformed and public services improved by breaking up existing monopolies and without overloading the third sector; and they suggest a model of risk transfer to the private and third sectors that could be used elsewhere throughout the welfare state.

The third area in which Compassionate Economics could transform the public sector lies in the way the state deals with people. As we discussed in Chapter 3, at present the state uses an operational model for delivery of public services which is based on a misreading of management theory and so an obsession with cost and cost-control. It attempts to depersonalise, segment and proceduralise all interactions with individual people; it fragments personal responsibility and accountability; and it insists on huge and cumbersome processes of verification and audit. The apparently paradoxical results are huge unexpected costs and waste, employee demoralisation and poorer outcomes.

This is, again, not a small topic for discussion. But, in line with Compassionate Economics, the direction of reform is clear. What is needed is to move towards seeing each strand of public service as a distinct institution, and specifically a complex system, in and of itself; to relax the present obsession with cost control in favour of a focus on quality; and to treat users and employees not merely as economically rational agents but as human beings.

If you look at any successful organisation, from Google to Toyota to Innocent Drinks, they are characterised by a relentless focus on improving the user's experience. Happy users ask very little of the organisations that serve them, so that "failure demand"—the stress imposed when something goes wrong—is kept to a minimum. The effect is that a focus on quality does not increase, but in fact minimises, long-run costs. Why should the British public sector be any different?

Between Public and Private

So far we have looked at how to make the private and public sectors work better. But Compassionate Economics is not just about existing institutions; it is also about new ones. One new institution which would offer enormous public benefit would be a British National Assets and Public Accountability Trust to manage key national assets at arm's length from government.

Recall that in textbook economics income and wealth are treated as equivalent. A stream of annual payments can be discounted back to a given lump sum amount, and the standard theory implies that we should be indifferent between the two. But applied to policy, this idea embodies a crucial and highly convenient fallacy. For it can be true—and it is often in fact true—both that the stream of payments and the lump sum are mathematically equivalent, and that they are radically different in their political and policy implications. A government oriented to national wealth will seek to protect and enhance its capital, and invest it in capital assets. An expenditure-oriented government will feel freer to use its capital for current spending. It will also feel freer to take on capital obligations today in the belief that these are simply streams of future expenditure whose funding later governments can be left to wrestle with.

Governments like to spend without taxing, and they like to promise capital sums without the unpleasant necessity of having to pay for them immediately. Over the past 30 years they have regularly felt free to do both. Under the Thatcher government, the proceeds of North Sea oil and of privatisation were largely incorporated into current spending. The same has happened under Blair and Brown, and to these proceeds have memorably been added much of the country's gold reserves and the £22 billion-plus receipts from the auction of 3G mobile telephone licences in 2001. On the other side of the public balance sheet, since 1997 there has been a huge build-up in public capital liabilities, notably for public pensions. It is no coincidence that there has also been a significant loss of interest in party politics among young people, who increasingly believe that the baby boomers have hijacked the Exchequer.

The Norwegians, however, have taken a different approach to their wealth. In 1997 they established the Government Pension Fund—Global, as a continuation of the Government Petroleum Fund set up in 1990. The initial capitalisation was NKr 48 billion. In every year since then the national accounts have shown a capital surplus, of which between 60% and 99% has been transferred to the fund. The fund has also grown through its own active and diversified financial management.

As a result, the Norwegians now have a fund with a value last year of NKr 2.02 trillion, roughly equivalent to £200 billion. It is controlled by the Norwegian Ministry of Finance, run by the national bank in four offices worldwide through expert independent money managers, and it is formally accountable to the Norwegian parliament. It is inexpensively managed. Its accounts are a model of jargon-free public explanation and transparency.

The fund has three functions. First, it manages the public oil and gas revenues of the country, as a capital resource for the benefit of future generations. Secondly, it manages the national bank's foreign exchange reserves. Thirdly, it manages a petroleum insurance fund, as a reserve to cover losses and liability arising from Norway's investments in oil and gas.

Norway is thus a huge worldwide investor. Unlike some purely financial investors it takes its ownership rights extremely seriously, following guidelines mandated by the Norwegian parliament. As a result, the fund increasingly holds companies in which it is invested directly accountable for their actions—in line with our emphasis above on improving corporate performance—and it publicly lists and will not invest in those that do not measure up. Such companies currently include Raytheon, Thales and Lockheed Martin (cluster munitions), Serco (involvement in nuclear weapons), Wal-Mart (breaches of human rights) and Freeport McMoRan (environmental damage). The US firm Kerr-McGee has been listed but subsequently readmitted.

The Norwegian approach has much to recommend it. It is successful, long-term, transparent, ethical and democratic. It gives Norway huge clout in the global capital markets, which it can and does use to encourage best practice. And it gives the Norwegian people a clear understanding of their national wealth and of the endowment that this generation will pass on to its successors, and so on. Nor does the fund fetter the hands of parliament. Parliament can change the formal purposes of the fund, or even dissolve it. The Ministry of Finance can transfer as much capital surplus as it chooses, when it chooses. The government can ultimately spend the capital assets just as it wishes, or has been democratically mandated.

So the real issue here is not economic, but political and moral. It is a matter of what constraints government should be under to account for its actions. Current spending of capital receipts is a free ride for politicians, in which they can costlessly mortgage the prospects of the next generation to satisfy the present one. It should not be. One function of a new UK National Assets and Public Accountability Trust would be to build proper transparency and debate into a crucial aspect of UK economic policy.

A trust of this kind does not fetter government. But it makes it more accountable. A finance minister who wishes to sell the country's gold reserves cannot simply act alone, but must (quickly and discreetly) make the argument—and be judged publicly on the consequences. A prime minister who wishes to spend using the trust's assets must explain why. A government which wishes to control or influence companies whose shares are held by the trust must set out its reasoning. After a huge windfall such as that from 3G mobile licence sales, there will be immediate pressure to add the new moneys to the national asset trust.

Over the years we have learned to be nervous about political interference in monetary policy. We have learned the value of new institutions such as the Lottery, which manage public resources semi-independently of government. So also now with national wealth.

And there is always the economic benefit to be considered. The accountants PWC have estimated that if the UK had invested its North Sea oil receipts in a national asset trust, the fund would now be worth £450 billion. That is the same as total UK tax revenues for 2007-8. Add in the £70 billion or so of UK privatisation proceeds, plus 3G mobile receipts and accumulated interest, and you would have well over £600 billion. Even outside the fund, the British economy would be stronger, since it would not have been artificially sustained by this enormous 30 year unearned capital flow.

The UK is heavily in debt at present, so setting up a national asset trust might seem premature. In fact, however, the exact opposite is true. The goal that it addresses, of ensuring greater fiscal transparency and accountability in British government, is an absolutely vital one. The value of such a fund lies not merely in the pool of wealth which it creates, but in the institution, and in the example of disciplined and accountable economic management, which it establishes. We need a new fiscal settlement in this country. New institutional means are required to create the necessary accountability, and this is one important move towards that goal. As with William III, we must make the executive more accountable to make it more trustworthy and effective.

And there is a more specific reason. The British government now owns the Northern Rock bank. It has just been forced to take significant, not to say controlling, stakes in Royal Bank of Scotland, Lloyds TSB and HBOS. Nominally, the government has little direct influence over the operations of these institutions. In reality, politicians, interest groups and the media have already begin to exert huge pressure for the government to push these institutions to make more politically helpful decisions over repossessions, credit and internal rationalisation. But while there needs to be a thorough overhaul of banking regulation, it is of vital importance to insulate the banking system from political interference during this process. What better way to launch a new national asset trust than by committing these assets into it, and ensuring the transparency and accountability that the system so conspicuously lacks at present?

These, then, are a few of the policy consequences of Compassionate Economics. They show its potential and range in action.

Wiser Government and the Future of Politics

It will not surprise the reader that the final thing we need is for government to become much wiser about the nature, use and value of economics itself. This does not simply involve a change of mind of a few key people at the top, and nor is it simply procedural. It will not be achieved purely by a change of political or administrative personnel within No. 10 Downing Street. On the contrary, if it is to be effective it requires a gigantic change in the beliefs and expectations of our public administration. The shift in institutional perspective must be very widely shared within government—including parliament, agencies, quangos and local government—and it must reflect a distinct, well-articulated and shared public conception of the new approach.

Much of what is needed here will focus on the detailed machinery of government, and includes such things as a thorough revamping of standard manuals, documents and procedures within the Civil Service; retraining of public officials, both those in technical positions and their "clients"; properly cautious and independent briefings for ministers on the likely effects of key decisions; and strengthening of the analytical capabilities of select committees.

But it also implies a different attitude on the part of our politicians. One of the lessons of the past ten years has been to remind us of the dangers of over-reliance on a certain kind of officially certified expertise. External consultants have proliferated. In many cases their supposed professional expertise does not actually embody genuine understanding. But even when it does, professional advisers are often far too uncritically used, to avoid responsibility rather than to inform decision-making. And the overall effect is to suggest that many genuinely political matters are in some sense "merely technical": to substitute economics for politics, and to relegate politics to the margin.

But this reflects a profound misunderstanding. Politics is a quintessentially amateur activity. Not amateurish, of course: it can always be carried on in a professional and competent way. But of its nature, it involves endless trade-offs between incommensurable priorities and values. Do you build this airport, or save this wilderness? Do you create these new hospitals, or put extra money into child support? Do you increase the state pension, or spend more on the armed forces and anti-terrorism measures? As soon as politicians adopt a particular professional viewpoint—be it that of businessman, the environmentalist, the doctor, the social worker, the soldier, or the economist—it becomes more difficult for them to strike the right balance. Expertise can only get you so far. More valuable by far are experience, wisdom, independent judgement—and common sense.

Among other things, then, Compassionate Economics provides a means by which to reintroduce common sense—about people, about institutions, about markets, and about the limits of government—back into British political debate. By challenging the present consensus in our public administration, it clears the way for new ideas, new energy and new creativity. Government is constrained and held properly accountable. New institutions and new voices are made possible. The people are empowered, they know more, and they prosper.

Acknowledgements

This short book is the second half of a broader project whose goal has been to set out a coherent intellectual and practical basis for the "New Conservatism". The first part, *Compassionate Conservatism* (2006; written with Janan Ganesh) looked at the historical traditions and philosophical ideas lying behind a British "compassionate conservatism". It described the idea of a "connected society", and argued that this required a shift in the basic categories developed in Anglo-American political theory since Hobbes—a reorientation away from a "vertical" preoccupation with the individual vs. the state, and towards a "horizontal" concern with society, institutions and human relationships. It then extended these ideas into an outline policy agenda.

Last year a shorter pamphlet, *From Here to Fraternity* (2007), applied these ideas to contemporary British politics, and explored the idea of fraternity in particular. It argued, against the prevailing wisdom, that the Conservative party had in fact seized the intellectual agenda and that, as a set of ideas, New Labour had reached the end of its useful life. Indeed, it showed how Gordon Brown and his party were caught in an impossible dilemma between political principle and political relevance. So, as later events have shown, they have proved to be.

Like its precursors, *Compassionate Economics* is not a work of politics, history, philosophy or indeed economics as such. It draws on related in-sights from these and other disciplines, and seeks to fashion out of them a distinct and coherent view of what our British political economy should be. It is not an instant book, rushed out in reaction to the crisis in the global financial system, though its ideas have some bearing on how to manage that crisis, and on the post-crisis economic world. It has been written entirely independently of any political party, and solely expresses the views of its author, and not those of Policy Exchange or of any other institution. Conservatives tend to be nervous about originality, so it may be a relief that very little in this book is original.

That said, I owe a huge amount to the work, advice and support of others. First and foremost is Oliver Hartwich, until recently Chief Economist of Policy Exchange, who helped to conceive the book and spent many hours arguing over it with me. Needless to say, he is not responsible for what remains. Many of those who helped with *Compassionate Conservatism* also influenced this book, and I thank them again. I am especially grateful to Anthony Browne and Neil O'Brien, successive Directors of Policy Exchange, and my colleagues there, especially Natalie Evans and Sam Freedman. I would also like to express my gratitude to John Adams, Lee Auspitz, Shamil Chandaria, Robert AG Monks, Bobby Monks, Torquil Norman, Casey Norman, Shefali Rai, Abi Senthilkumaran, Scott Sturgeon and several anonymous academic and other readers. Policy Exchange and I are grateful for the financial support provided by the Hadley Trust. A special thanks yet again to my beloved wife Kate Bingham and Sam, Nell and Noah Norman—without whom not.

Readers who would like to discuss these issues are welcome to contact me by email on jesse.norman@policyexchange.org.uk.

Endnotes

In the text we deliberately use some shortcuts for reasons of simplicity or readability. Thus we use "conventional economics", "textbook economics", "economism", "rigor mortis economics" and the like interchangeably except where the difference is relevant. The same is true for "the UK" and "GB". However, we distinguish between big-C "Conservatives", who are affiliated to that party; and "conservatives", who may in principle belong to any political party, or to none. Classic works of economics or philosophy are not cited.

Introduction

Bank of England: *Financial Stability Report*, October 2008

Francis Fukuyama: *The End of History and the Last Man,* Penguin, 1992

Chapter 1: The British Economy: Miracle or Mirage?

Relative real GDP growth: *National Accounts of OECD Countries*, OECD

Population growth since 1992: *Population Trends,* Office of National Statistics

Rise in house prices: *Nationwide House Price Index*, Nationwide, April 2008

Current savings rate: Office of National Statistics, June 2008

Equity withdrawal: *Housing Equity Withdrawal,* Bank of England

Public spending and waste: David Craig, *Squandered*, Constable, 2008

Immigration: *The Economic Impact of Immigration*, House of Lords, April 2008

Thatcher government and the state: Simon Jenkins, *Accountable to None*, Hamish Hamilton 1995; *Thatcher and Sons*, Allen Lane, 2006

Gordon Brown on productivity: Pre-Budget Report speech 1997, *Pre-Budget Report*, 1998

Government productivity report: *The Sunday Times,* April 2004

NHS productivity: "Take Your Pick", *Economist*, 4 March 2006

Negative impact of public spending on GDP growth: David B. Smith, *Living with Leviathan,* IEA, 2006, Ch. 3

OECD study: *Programme for International Student Assessment* (PISA), 2006

Green Book: HM Treasury, *The Green Book: Appraisal and Evaluation in Central Government*

Tax credits: House of Commons Public Accounts Committee, *Tax Credits and PAYE Eighth Report*, 2008

Single parents claiming tax credits: Frank Field, "Blame faulty tax credits for bad behaviour", *Daily Telegraph*, 3 October 2007

Chapter 2: A Fracture in Society

Social decline: for detailed analysis of these issues see in particular the work of Iain Duncan-Smith and the Centre for Social Justice

Drug use: European Monitoring Centre for Drugs and Drug Addiction, *Annual Report,* 2005

Binge drinking: Institute of Alcohol Studies *"Binge Drinking" Fact Sheet*, 2006

Teenage births: *Innocenti Report Card*, UNICEF Innocenti Centre, July 2001

Children in workless households: *Monitoring Poverty and Social Exclusion in the UK 2005*, Joseph Rowntree Foundation

UNICEF report: *Childhood in Industrialised Countries*, UNICEF, February 2007

NEETs: *The Cost of Exclusion: Counting the Cost of Youth Disadvantage in the UK*, Prince's Trust and RBS, April 2007

Child obesity: *Health Profiles*, Association of Public Health Observatories, June 2008

Voting patterns: *Power to the People*, The POWER Inquiry, February 2006

Excesses of consumerism: see e.g. Benjamin Barber, *Consumed*, Norton, 2007

Clone Towns: *Clone Town Britain*, New Economics Foundation, 2005

Mill on economics: "On the Definition of Political Economy", in *Essays on Some Unsettled Questions of Political Economy*, 1964

Samuelson: Paul Samuelson and William Nordhaus, *Economics*, McGraw-Hill, 2004

Public Choice theory: James Buchanan and Gordon Tullock, *The Calculus of Consent*, University of Michigan Press 1962; see also Gordon Tullock, *The Vote Motive,* IEA 1976/2006

Kahneman and Tversky: see e.g. Daniel Kahneman, Paul Slovic and Amos Tversky, Judgement Under Uncertainty, Cambridge University Press, 1982; and Daniel Kahneman and Amos Tversky, *Choices, Values and Frames*, Cambridge University Press, 2000

Gary Becker: see e.g. *The Economics of Discrimination*, University of Chicago Press, 1957/1971

George Akerlof: see e.g. "The Market for 'Lemons': Quality Uncertainty and the Market Mechanism", *Quarterly Journal of Economics,* August 1970

Chapter 3: Rigor Mortis Economics

Efficient markets: see e.g. Andrei Shleifer, *Inefficient Markets*, Oxford University Press, 2000; John Kay, *The Truth About Markets*, Allen Lane, 2003 and references.

Welfare and imperfect information: see Joseph Stiglitz, *Whither Socialism?*, MIT Press, 1994

Behavioural economics: see e.g. the Kahneman/Tversky collections above; and Richard Thaler and Cass Sunstein, *Nudge*, Yale University Press, 2008. For an up-to-date summary of the field, see Nick Wilkinson, *An Introduction to Behavioral Economics*, Palgrave Macmillan, 2008

Baumol's Cost Disease: William J. Baumol and William G. Bowen, *Performing Arts: The Economic Dilemma*, Twentieth Century Fund,

1966. For recent empirical support across a variety of sectors see "Baumol's Diseases: A Macroeconomic Perspective", William D. Nordhaus, *NBER Working Paper* 12218, May 2006

Operational models: see John Seddon, *Systems Thinking in the Public Sector*, Triarchy Press, 2008; also Chris Dillow, *The End of Politics*, Harriman House, 2007

Willingness to pay, and risk: John Adams, *Risk*, UCL Press, 1995

Chapter 4: The Danger of Happiness

Theory X and Theory Y: see Douglas McGregor, *The Human Side of Enterprise*, McGraw-Hill, 1960/2006. Quoted in Seddon 2008

Layard: Richard Layard, *Happiness: Lessons from a New Science*, Allen Lane, 2005

Sen on capability: see Amartya Sen, "Capability and Wellbeing" and the other papers in Amartya Sen and Martha Nussbaum (eds), *The Quality of Life,* Oxford University Press, 1993

Neuroscience of compassion: see in particular the work of Jean Decety and collaborators, via http://home.uchicago.edu/~decety/jean_cv.html. E.g. "A Social-Neuroscience Perspective on Empathy", *Current Directions in Psychological Science*, 15.2

"Battery" children: C. Norton, "After a century, we've produced the stressed-out cooped up battery children of today", *The Independent*, 2 September 1999

High trust/low trust environments: D. Knoch et al., "Diminishing reciprocal fairness by disrupting the right prefrontal cortex", *Science* 314, 2006

Volunteering: *The Health Benefits of Volunteering: A Review of Recent Research*, Corporation for National and Community Service, 2007; also e.g. Allan Luks and Peggy Payne, *The Healing Power of Doing Good*, iUniverse.com, 2001

Knights, knaves, pawns, queens: Julian LeGrand, *Motivation, Agency and Public Policy,* Oxford University Press, 2003

Ofsted report on maths: *Mathematics: Understanding the Score*, Ofsted, September 2008

OECD school hours: *Education at a Glance 2008: OECD Indicators*, OECD, September 2008

Chapter 5: The Social Foundations of Economic Prosperity

Impact of William III: see Tim Harford, *The Logic of Life*, Little Brown, 2008, citing (among others) Douglass North and Barry Weingast, "Constitutions and Commitment: the Evolution of Institutions Governing Public Choice in Seventeenth Century England", *Journal of Economic History* 49.4, 1989; and Harry Bingham, *This Little Britain*, Fourth Estate, 2007

Entrepreneurship: see e.g. Israel Kirzner, *Competition and Entrepreneurship*, University of Chicago Press, 1973; and Jesus Huerta de Soto, *The Austrian School*, Edward Elgar, 2008

Chapter 6: Compassionate Economics

Failed safeguards: Martin Wolf, "What the British authorities should try now", *Financial Times*, 31 October 2008

CEO compensation: Polly Toynbee and David Walker, *Unjust Rewards*, Granta Books, 2008

Importance of owners: the modern literature on this is enormous, but see e.g. Robert Monks and Allen Sykes, *Capitalism without Owners Will Fail*, CSFI, November 2002

Directors as fiduciaries, not agents: Robert C. Clark, *Agency Costs vs. Fiduciary Duties*, in John Pratt and Richard Zeckhauser (eds.) *Principals and Agents*, Harvard Business School Press, 1985

McKinsey study: *A New Era in Governance,* McKinsey Quarterly 2, 2004

ISS study: Lawrence Brown and Marcus Caylor, *The Correlation between Corporate Governance and Company Performance*, Institutional Shareholder Services, 2004

Deutsche Bank study: *Beyond the Numbers: Corporate Governance in the UK*, Deutsche Bank, February 2004

Incapacity benefit reform: see e.g. David Freud, *Reducing Dependency, Increasing Opportunity: Options for the Future of Welfare to Work*, Department of Work and Pensions, 2007; and the long-term Payment by Results work of the Shadow DWP team

Schools reform: see Michael Gove, "Parents should be able to choose schools instead of schools choosing parents", *ConservativeHome*, 7 July 2008

Norwegian sovereign wealth fund: *Norges Bank Investment Management Annual Report 2007,* Norges Bank

About the Author

Jesse Norman is a Senior Fellow and former Executive Director of Policy Exchange. He was a director at Barclays before leaving the City in 1997 to research and teach at University College London. He was educated at Oxford University (BA) and at UCL (MPhil, PhD), where he holds an honorary research fellowship in philosophy. His books include *Compassionate Conservatism* (with Janan Ganesh), *The Achievement of Michael Oakeshott* (ed.), *Breaking the Habits of a Lifetime* and *After Euclid*, and he has written widely in the national press. A lifelong volunteer, among other things he is a main board director of The Roundhouse in London and of the Hay Festival. In 2006 he was adopted as Conservative parliamentary candidate for Hereford and South Herefordshire.

www.jessenorman.com

University of Buckingham Press

About The University of Buckingham Press

The University of Buckingham Press is the publishing arm of the only independent university in the UK. It publishes and distributes authoritative independent research and academic works in books and journals.